Transfiction

Characters in Search of Translation Studies

Edited by

Marko Miletich

SUNY Buffalo State University

Series in Literary Studies

VERNON PRESS

www.vernonpress.com

In the Americas:	*In the rest of the world:*
Vernon Press	Vernon Press
1000 N West Street, Suite 1200	C/Sancti Espiritu 17,
Wilmington, Delaware, 19801	Malaga, 29006
United States	Spain

Series in Literary Studies

Library of Congress Control Number: 2023946585

ISBN: 978-1-64889-939-3

Also available: 978-1-64889-790-0 [Hardback]; 978-1-64889-812-9 [PDF, E-Book]

Cover design by Vernon Press using elements designed by rawpixel.com / Freepik and benzoix / Freepik.

All characters appearing in these chapters are fictitious. Any resemblance to real professionals is not coincidental and is meant to be utilized for didactic purposes.

Table of Contents

List of Acronyms   vii

About the Authors   ix

Acknowledgments   xiii

Introduction   xv
Marko Miletich
SUNY Buffalo State University

Chapter 1   **Diego Marani's Interpreters, Linguists,**
             Lawbreakers and Loonies   1
             Marella Feltrin-Morris
             Ithaca College

Chapter 2   **The Interpreter's Visibility and Agency in Yuri**
             Herrera's *Signs Preceding the End of the World*   17
             Caragh Barry
             University of California, Santa Barbara

Chapter 3   **Intervention as a Form of Survival:**
             Suki Kim's *The Interpreter*   35
             Irem Ayan
             The University of British Columbia

Chapter 4   **Unbearable Intimacies: The Implicated**
             Interpreter in Katie Kitamura's *Intimacies*   51
             Yan Wu
             University of Massachusetts Amherst

Chapter 5   **Translator (In)Visibility in Rodolfo Walsh's**
             "La aventura de las pruebas de imprenta"   69
             Marko Miletich
             SUNY Buffalo State University

Chapter 6   **Translation and Creative Writing:
            Anita Desai's "Translator Translated"**   87

Sheela Mahadevan
King's College London

Afterthoughts   105

Marko Miletich
SUNY Buffalo State University

Index   109

List of Acronyms

AIIC	Association International des Interprètes de Conférence
EEAS	European External Action Service
INS	Immigration and Naturalization Service
NAJIT	National Association of Judiciary Interpreters and Translators
NeMLA	Northeast Modern Language Association
OCR	Optical Character Recognition

About the Authors

Irem Ayan

Assistant Professor of Traductology and Translation, University of British Columbia

Irem Ayan holds an MA in Conference Interpreting from Institut libre Marie Haps in Brussels and a Ph.D. in Translation Studies from Binghamton University as a Fulbright scholar. Her research interests include interpreting, race and gender in interpreting, the sociology and (auto)ethnography of interpreting, and fictional representations of translators and interpreters. In her book manuscript tentatively entitled *The Emotional Labor of Conference Interpreting: Gender, Alienation and Sabotage*, she explores how interpreters assume another "I" by performing various forms of emotional labor and how this holds important consequences for interpreters' sense of identity, including gender. She also investigates the unreasonable and abominable situations such as gender-based discrimination, mistreatment, exploitation, and harassment of various kinds with which interpreters need to deal in various contexts of their work. She is also a practicing conference interpreter, with experience and training within several international organizations such as the United Nations in New York and the European Union and NATO in Brussels.

Caragh Barry

PhD in Hispanic Literature, University of California, Santa Barbara

Caragh Barry is a translator, interpreter, and Spanish language instructor at the University of California, Santa Barbara. Her research explores the intersections of translation and interpretation with fiction, gender, identity, class, and emotion in works such as Andrés Neuman's *Viajero del siglo*, Yuri Herrera's *Señales que precederán al fin del mundo*, and Valeria Luiselli's works of both fiction and nonfiction, among others. Barry's most recent academic work has appeared in *Dedalus* (Portugal, 2022) and *Review: Literature and Arts of the Americas* (2020). In addition to her academic and teaching work, Barry translates both prose and poetry from Spanish and Portuguese. Her translations of Manoel de Barros and Úrsula Fuentesberain have appeared, respectively, in *Virada* (2019) and *Latin American Literature Today* (2018), and a novel-length translation of Luke Hernández Martín is forthcoming.

Marella Feltrin-Morris

Professor of Italian, Ithaca College

Marella Feltrin-Morris has published articles on translation, paratext, and pedagogy, as well as on modern and contemporary Italian literature. Among her recent publications are "A First Taste of Translation: Introducing Context" (in the volume *Spunti e riflessioni per una didattica della traduzione e dell'interpretariato nelle SSML,* edited by Valeria Petrocchi, Edizioni CompoMat, 2022) and "Welcome Intrusions: Capturing the Unexpected in Translators' Prefaces to Dante's *Divine Comedy*" (*Tusaaji: A Translation Review,* 2018). Her translations of short stories by Luigi Pirandello, Massimo Bontempelli, and Paola Masino have appeared in *North American Review, Two Lines, Exchanges,* and *Green Mountains Review,* among other journals. She is a contributor to the collaborative digital edition *Stories for a Year,* an ongoing project that will provide the first complete English translation of Pirandello's short stories. To date, nineteen of her translations of Pirandello's short stories have been published in *Stories for a Year.*

Sheela Mahadevan

King's College London

Sheela Mahadevan holds a Ph.D. in French and Comparative literature from King's College London, funded by the UK Arts and Humanities Research Council. She was the recipient of a UK-Canada Globalink Award for research into literary translation at Concordia University, Montreal (2021-2022), and was awarded scholarships for French translation residencies at the British Centre for Literary Translation (2021) and Bristol University, UK (2022). She has taught French literary translation and Comparative Literature at King's College London. Her research on translation and multilingualism has been published in *Asymptote,* a journal of translation and world literature, and her English translation of Ari Gautier's Indian Francophone novel *Carnet secret de Lakshmi* (Lakshmi's Secret Diary) is forthcoming with Columbia University Press in 2024.

Marko Miletich

Assistant Professor of Spanish, Translation and Interpreting, Buffalo State University

Marko Miletich obtained a Ph.D. in Translation Studies from Binghamton University in 2012. He has an MA in liberal arts with a Concentration in Translation from the City University of New York (CUNY) Graduate Center and an MA in Hispanic Civilization from New York University. He has worked extensively as a professional translator and interpreter and has developed curricula for several courses in translation, as well as serving as a coordinator for Translation and Interpretation programs. He has published articles about gender issues in translation, service-learning, non-verbal communication in interpreting, and transfiction. His literary translations have appeared in *Reunion: The Dallas Review* and *KIN Online Literary Translation Journal.* Marko Miletich also served as editor for this volume.

Yan Wu

Ph.D. candidate in Comparative Literature Program at the University of Massachusetts, Amherst

Yan Wu received her MA with Merit in Conference Interpreting and Translation Studies from the University of Leeds and her MA in Applied Linguistics from Anhui University. Her research and teaching interests include translation and migration, translation and multilingualism, history of interpreting, translation theory, life writing, and eco-fiction. Her ongoing dissertation project focuses on reading the figure of the interpreter as an analytical category in Chinese diasporic literature. Her publications are to appear in *Translating Home in the Global South: Migration, Belonging, and Language Justice* and a special issue on the "Translation Memoir" in *Life Writing.* She is also a certified interpreter and translator (CATTI Level II&I) and a winner of the Han Suyin Award for Literary Translators in 2017. Besides her academic pursuits, she works as a freelance interpreter in various community and conference settings.

Acknowledgments

The inspiration for this book originated during a panel on transfiction at the 2022 Northeast Modern Language Association (NeMLA) in Baltimore, Maryland. I would like to thank NeMLA for their continuous inclusion of topics related to translation studies.

Editing a book is harder than I thought and more rewarding than I could have ever imagined. This volume would not have been possible without the help and support of several people. I am extremely grateful for their assistance and encouragement.

I would like to thank my friend and colleague, Dr. José Dávila Montes, for his support and advice for this project (and throughout my career). I would like to thank my colleague at Buffalo State University (SUNY), Dr. Mark Warford, for his insightful comments and positive feedback. I would also like to thank Dr. Erin Riddle for her careful editing and expertise.

I am eternally grateful to my former thesis director, mentor, and friend, Dr. Carrol Coates, who taught me to persevere in times of difficulty and how to read carefully. Unknowingly, he contributed to the planning and conceptualization of this volume long before the project was initiated.

I would like to thank the authors for contributing to this volume, a truly international group: Irem Ayan, Caragh Barry, Marella Feltrin-Morris, Sheela Mahadevan, and Yan Wu. They kept to the strict deadlines and worked diligently to write, submit, and revise their chapters. Thank you for sharing your expertise and providing a great service to our field.

Finally, on behalf of all my colleagues, I would especially like to express my gratitude to the publishing company, Vernon Press, for giving us the opportunity to publish this volume. Special thanks to the editor at Vernon Press, Blanca Caro Durán, who patiently answered all my questions and addressed my concerns through many online meetings. This book would not have been possible without her expert guidance through the publishing process.

Introduction

Marko Miletich

SUNY Buffalo State University

> As it is with a play, so it is with life — what matters is not
> how long the acting lasts, but how good it is.
>
> Seneca

Fiction is a lie. Transfiction is a double lie.

The short stories and novels we read are not real. We are aware of this fact, and yet, we "like reading fiction because it lets us try on different mental states and seems to provide intimate access to the thoughts, intentions, and feelings of other people in our social environment" (Zunshine, 2006, p. 25). Fiction (re)creates a world readers can visit with the help of the words in a text and their imagination. The tales we read often include people living in worlds similar to their human counterparts. These putative beings serve as stand-ins for our everyday flesh-and-blood lives and psychological conundrums. Sometimes, these fabricated beings (re)present predetermined social norms and expectations for certain professions (such as doctors, teachers, writers, and, in our case, translators and interpreters). Such fictional characters often provide insights into the experiences of such professionals and the worlds they inhabit.

Transfiction–a term used to describe the portrayal of translation (as both a topic and a motif) as well as translators and interpreters in fiction and film–is also a lie.[1] Those depictions are not true; they are immersed in an imaginary literary existence. Fictional translations utilized in short stories and novels

---

[1] The term *Transfiction* has also been used to define a mixed-reality system where users can be transported into fictional spaces via virtual reality through the user's appearance or its avatar. *Transfictionality* is also currently used to describe the transfer of an established literary character into a new fiction that differs from the original fiction. *Trans Fiction* (two separate words) is applied to the literary production that addresses, has been written by, or portrays people of diverse gender identities. Throughout this volume, the term *Transfiction* will refer to the use of translation and translators/interpreters in fiction. *Transfictional* is the adjective used to describe these types of stories.

never really existed, and neither do the imagined language professionals who reside in these fictitious stories. However, fantastical characters do face situations and challenges that serve to represent the everyday lives and mental states of their real live counterparts. Transfiction also serves as an invaluable pedagogical tool for discussing the intricate world of translation studies and its many sub-areas. Several translation scholars (Arrojo, 2018 & Kaindl, 2014, among others referenced in this volume) have discussed the benefits of using fiction as a teaching tool for translator and interpreter training. These transfictional tales can be utilized to introduce translation theories, examine sociological aspects of translation (expectations of the translator/interpreter, their positionality within a particular society, and ideological, political, and social areas of conflict), and discuss translatorial behavior and strategies (Kaindl, 2018, p. 164).

Translation has often been viewed as a derivative activity (an act of simple reproduction), while the writing of originals is considered to be a creative activity (a unique production) (Chamberlain, 1988). Translators, therefore, have been seen as servile, often nameless scribes who become invisible as they (re)write the words of another. Contemporary fictional translators and interpreters, however, are no longer seen as "mere interlingual photocopiers, but [as] beings that live and operate in complex sociocultural contexts" (Miletich, 2018, p. 175). Fictional texts that include translators and interpreters as characters "represent a discursive vehicle for highlighting the presence rather than the absence of the translator" (Wilson, 2007, p. 393).

Certainly, ideas regarding translation as mere transference of static meaning and once expressed in musical terms (as echoes), painting terms (as copies or portraits), or as sartorial terms (as borrowed or ill-fitting clothing) have been mostly defunct for some time; however, followers of traditional views of translation still cling to the idea of the translator/interpreter as a secondary and invisible being who should not intervene in any considerable way. Modern scholarship, nevertheless, "requires that we bring the translator [and the interpreter] as a social being fully into the picture" (Hermans, 1996, p. 26). The transformation of a statement or a text from one language to another through the mediating actions of an interpreter or translator leaves evidence of an unavoidable existence. All acts of translation and interpreting require intervention. The translator/interpreter's presence and intervention are inevitable (both in translations and interpreter-mediated events), as the chapters herein amply demonstrate.

Over the last few decades, there has been a considerable increase in the presence of translation as a topic and motif, including translators and interpreters as protagonists in literature and film. The reason for this surge, notes Klaus Kaindl (2014), is that "literature and film are never detached from society, but rather react to its developments, changes and upheavals with their own methods and devices" (p. 4). Consequently, translation studies scholars began to explore the potential of fiction to discuss theoretical aspects of interpreting and translation. Subsequently, translation studies started to witness a "fictional turn"–a label first developed by Brazilian scholar Else Vieira (1995), who encouraged "the incorporation of fictional-theoretical parameters" (p. 51). In fact, "the study of fiction as a source of translation theorization was no doubt one of the main contributions to translation theory in the 1990s (Pagano, 2002, p. 81). Transfiction research continues to grow in importance in the twenty-first century. Transfiction, therefore, is a pillar of this "fictional turn" since it represents "an aestheticized imagination of translatorial action" (Spitzl, 2014, p. 364) and a venue to explore the intricacies of translation and interpreting, as well as the task of interpreters and translators.

Interest in transfiction as a subfield of translation studies gave rise to the "First International Conference on Fictional Translators in Literature and Film," which took place at the University of Vienna Centre for Translation Studies in September 2011. The conference produced a series of articles analyzing the intersection of translation and fiction, which were subsequently published in a special issue of the journal *Linguistica Antverpiensia, New Series–Themes in Translation Studies* (issue 4) in 2005. Two other conferences followed: "Translators and (Their) Authors" at Tel-Aviv University in 2013 and "The Fictions of Translation" at Concordia University in Montreal, 2015, which produced a collection of essays edited by Judith Woodsworth under the title *The Fictions of Translation* (2018). Recently, the Northeast Modern Language Association's (NeMLA) annual convention has featured panels on transfiction. In 2022, NeMLA included a panel entitled "Transfiction: The Fictional Eye of Translation Studies" (which resulted in several chapters in this collection). That convention was held in Baltimore, Maryland. The following year, 2023, the convention in Niagara Falls, New York, featured a panel entitled "Fictional Translators: Exploring Translation Theory Trough Literature and Film." Transfiction, therefore, has proven to be a productive avenue for translation research. It has enabled a multidisciplinary perspective that includes a variety of fields such as anthropology, comparative literature, cultural studies, gender studies, history, and postcolonial studies, among others. Transfiction also serves a means for investigating social phenomena, as underscored in the stories analyzed in this volume.

Several contemporary writers have used translation as a theme in their fictional writing, while others have included translators and interpreters as characters. While fictional translation can contribute to the construction of a story, the inclusion of translators and interpreters as main or significant characters can be used to highlight aspects of the profession. These fictional beings function as protagonists, antagonists, helpers, or enemies. Some fiction writers have recognized the importance of translation as well as translators/interpreters, as a driving force of their plots. Hans Christian Hagedorn (2006) reminds us that, since the second half of the twentieth century, fictional translators have played more visible roles; they no longer occupy a marginal position but are becoming important characters or protagonists as an integral part of the narrative framework (p. 210).

Translation in fiction has been used as a vehicle for mystery. One of the most celebrated novels in Western literature is *Don Quixote* (2013/1605). The narrative highlights translation as a major theme since, as Miguel de Cervantes Saavedra's narrator tells us, the story is, in fact, a translation of an Arabic text written by Cide Hamete Benengeli and then translated by an unnamed Moor. This fictitious translation often questions the accuracy of the target text since the fictional translator himself is seen as untrustworthy, which is tied to concepts related to the "supposedly" intrinsic infidelity in translation. Nevertheless, it is thanks to a translator (imaginary as he might be) that the fabulous adventures of an outdated knight errant, obsessed with tales of chivalry, have been read by millions throughout the centuries.

Many famous fictional translators and interpreters have captured the attention of readers around the world, and recent fictional works have presented readers with examples of extreme essentialism, including Pierre Menard in Borges's "Pierre Menard, Author of the Quixote;"[2] the unethical practices of Ermes Marana in Italo Calvino's *If on a Winter's Night a Traveler;* the kleptomaniac tendencies of Gallus in Dezső Kosztolányi's *Kornél Esti;* the suicidal translators in Banana Yoshimoto's *NP;* the lesbian translator and part-time detective, Cassandra Reilly, in Barbara Wilson's *Gaudí Afternoon;* the historical figures La Malinche and Jerónimo de Aguilar made into fictitious characters as competing interpreters in Carlos Fuentes's *The Two Shores;* and Juan, the obnoxious interpreter/narrator in Javier Marías' *A Heart so White.* These are only a few examples, though there are numerous from which to choose, and several interesting fictional translators and interpreters receive scholarly attention in this volume.

The current collection of essays, *Transfiction: Characters in Search of Translation Studies,* seeks to complement previous work on transfiction. It explores recent fictional portrayals of translation, translators, and interpreters in fiction as a framework for inquiry into issues, concepts, and themes related

---

[2] Translation studies scholar George Steiner (1998) describes Borges's short story "Pierre Menard, Author of the Quixote"–an homage to Cervantes's novel and its fictional hidalgo–as the "most concentrated commentary anyone has offered on the business of translation" (p. 73).

to translation studies. Chapters in this volume include studies of translatorial acts and several language professionals (translators, interpreters, editors). Three chapters explore translation as the product of interpretive and creative processes (1, 5, & 6), and two examine translators (5, & 6), while interpreters are portrayed in four chapters (1, 2, 3, & 4). The greater presence of interpreters in the collection is due to the fact that these language professionals are more prominent in fiction. Fictional interpreters lend themselves to proximal human interaction (and the potential conflicts that this entails), while translators usually lead a more solitary existence. For that reason, interpreters are featured more frequently in fiction. Nevertheless, both translators and interpreters are at center stage in the following pages as characters with traits that define them socially, emotionally, and psychologically as complex individuals.

The essays in this volume touch upon a diverse range of subjects, but a common thread uniting all chapters is the topic of (in)visibility as analyzed through the act of translation and the fictional translators and interpreters who carry out the work. In addition, the volume also explores issues associated with agency, editing, ethics, (in)fidelity, gender, impartiality, manipulation, power struggles, translatability, and writing. Furthermore, the collection created an additional thread regarding the translator/interpreter functioning as a detective (chapters 1, 3, & 5).

All writers in this volume are either established scholars or advanced doctoral students writing their dissertations. These scholarly essays originate from a formidable group of academics writing about translation, interpretation, translators, and/or interpreters working in various languages (French, Italian, Korean, Oriya, and Spanish) and discuss the works of authors from different national backgrounds (Argentina, Italy, Korea, United States, Mexico, and India).

The collection starts with a reflection on language and language professionals by Marella Feltrin-Morris as she discusses three novels by Diego Marani: *New Finnish Grammar* (2000), *The Last of the Vostyachs* (2002), and *The Interpreter* (2004). Feltrin-Morris analyzes the author's thematic approach to language as an object of study, a creation, and an obsession. The idea of the "mother" tongue and the relationship, at times problematic, between language and identity is explored in these novels. The detective-like search for an idyllic pre-Babelian language aids Feltrin-Morris's inquiry into the portrayal of translators and interpreters, what their occupations relate to the meaning of language and the quest for a protolanguage. In addition, the chapter examines the lifespan and death of languages, language prestige, the benefits and detriments of translation, and the representation of translation as an act of violence.

Caragh Barry presents a thoughtful discussion on the agency of the interpreter and societal judgments regarding interpreter intervention for an intended outcome. She examines Yuri Herrera's *Signs Preceding the End of the World* (2015), a novella that portrays the United States-Mexico border and its dangerous crossing. The role of the interpreter is fundamental for those traversing territories, and Barry links the fictional interpreter in the story to the real flesh and blood historical figure La Malinche, comparing the struggles both characters face in navigating multiple words and loyalties. Barry further uses the novella to examine the power relations exercised in interpretation, negative interpreter depictions, and the reasons for and consequences of interpreting "unfaithfully." In addition, she analyzes the protagonist's Malinche-esque character to explore the central role of an interpreter in the migrant community.

The world of legal interpreting is probed by Irem Ayan as she discusses Suki Kim's *The Interpreter* (2003). Ayan examines how an interpreter's code of ethics buried beneath the surface of a seemingly impartial and invisible interpreter can be subverted. Gender becomes an important aspect of the novel as Ayan illustrates how interpreting is often seen as a feminized occupation, with Kim's story as an example of the interpreter's work understood through tropes of gendered and marginalized labor. The chapter also exposes how interpreters are often relegated to a secondary, subservient, and derivative role, often performing a form of emotional labor (managing emotions during interactions in interpreter-mediated events). Ayan also utilizes the text to call attention to power struggles that take place in depositions and other court settings. Additionally, her chapter describes interpreting as a sort of detective-like work since the protagonist sets out to investigate the murder mystery of her parents, thanks to one of her assignments.

Yan Wu also analyzes interpreter behavior as she introduces Katie Kitamura's *Intimacies* (2021). Within the setting of the International Criminal Court in The Hague and an interpreter working at an international war crime tribunal, Wu uses the novel to explore the intimate nature of interpreting as it is manifested through repeated face-to-face encounters in a common space of linguistic and physical proximity. Her analysis also considers the surrendering of the interpreter's personal "I" to an "alien I", since the first-person pronoun is used professionally in interpreter-mediated events. Wu considers the way in which Kitamura's text complicates the normative expectations for the interpreter's role as the invisible and neutral conduit. In addition, Wu examines depictions of the power dynamics surrounding interpreting activities and the traditional view of the profession as secondary and subservient labor. The chapter also examines the emotionally taxing task of interpreting at International Criminal Courts for war crime criminals.

Marko Miletich explores Rodolfo Walsh's "*La aventura de las pruebas de imprenta*" [The Adventure of the Printing Proofs] (1981), which offers a glimpse of the publishing industry and introduces a language professional who serves as a textual detective for this fascinating whodunit. The death of a translator serves to generate a discussion about translation and editing. Printing proofs and editor's marks become the center piece of the story as Miletich examines their importance in the publishing of translations and their intrinsic visibility. The chapter also provides a view of the publishing world, the publishing process, and the roles of translators and editors in that industry. The chapter, moreover, discusses the contradistinction between visibility and invisibility in translation. The chapter additionally reflects on how Walsh's story serves to establish a connection between the work of translators, editors, and detectives, as they all utilize observation and deductive skills to accomplish their tasks.

The relationship between translation and creative writing is chosen by Sheela Mahadevan as she examines Anita Desai's novella *Translator Translated* (2012). Mahadevan uses the text to analyze the intersections and similarities between translation and the writing processes. She exhibits *Translator Translated* to discuss the way in which the roles of translation and writing processes may intersect and mutually engage with one another. Mahadevan also examines what encourages translators to cross the boundaries between translation and creative writing. The chapter also serves to explore the impact of hegemonic languages (in this case, English) and the dominating role they play over minority languages (here Hindi, Oriya). Desai's text also interrogates the prestigious status of English literature as it compares to the precarious status of the indigenous literature of India. Mahadevan also illustrates the obvious connection between multilingual writing and literary translation and how the latter can provide a sense of renewal and rebirth for authors. Additionally, this chapter describes how the embellishment of a source text can transgress the conventional boundaries of translation.

The chapters in this collection reinforce the value and contributions of translation, interpreting, translators, and interpreters. Translation and interpreting are much more than the seemingly effortless "transfer" of oral or textual information. Translation on a quotidian basis (to acquire information, obtain knowledge, learn about other cultures, read literature, deal with political issues, communicate with people who speak different languages, and buy and sell products) makes the field of translation studies a crucial one in the twenty-first century. Furthermore, transfiction is a remarkable and enjoyable way to explore the fields of translation and interpreting so fundamental to everyday human interactions and exchange.

Translation and interpreting are more than mere "echoes," more than a faceless repetition of a previously written or spoken passage inaccessible outside the original language; translators and interpreters, unlike the nymph, do not waste away until their very bones turn into stone.[3] Indeed, translators and interpreters are language professionals omnipresent in their translatorial endeavors. Just as Luigi Pirandelo's characters in *Six Characters in Search of an Author* search for an author, the transfictional stories included in this collection can help us (re)search approaches to translation studies.

References

Arrojo, R. (2018). *Fictional translators: Rethinking translation through literature.* Routledge.

Borges, J. L. (1998). Pierre Menard author of the Quixote. In J. L. Borges, *Collected fictions by Jorge Luis Borges* (A. Hurley, Trans., pp. 88-95). Penguin Books.

Calvino, I. (1979). *If on a winter's night a traveler* (W. Weaver, Trans.). Harcourt.

Chamberlain, L. (1988). Gender and the metaphorics of translation. *Signs, 13*(3), 454-472.

de Cervantes Saavedra, M. (2013). *Don Quixote* (E. Grossman, Trans.). Harper Collins Publishers. (Original work published 1605).

Desai, A. (2012). Translator translated. In *The artist of disappearance* (pp. 41–92). Vintage.

Fuentes, C. (1994). The two shores. In C. Fuentes, *The orange tree* (A. MacAdam, Trans., pp. 3-50). Farrar, Straus and Giraux.

Hagedorn, H. C. (2006) *La traducción narrada: el recurso narrativo de la traducción ficticia.* Cuenca: Ediciones de la Universidad de Castilla-La Mancha.

Hermans, T. (1996). Norms and determination: A theoretical framework. In R. Álvarez, & C. Á. Vidal (Eds.), *Translation, Power, Subversion* (pp. 25-51). Multilingual Matters.

Herrera, Y. (2015). *Signs preceding the end of the world* (L. Dillman, Trans.). And other stories.

Kaindl, K. (2104). Going fictional! Translators and interpreters in literature and film: An introduction. In K. Kaindl, & K. Splitz (Eds.), *Transfiction: Research into the realities of translation fiction* (pp. 1-26). John Benjamins Publishing Company.

Kaindl, K. (2018). The remaking of the translator's reality: The role of fiction in translation studies. In J. Woodsworth (Ed.), *The fictions of translation* (pp. 157-170). John Benjamins Publishing Company.

Kim, S. (2003). *The Interpreter.* Picador.

Kitamura, K. M. (2021). *Intimacies.* Riverhead Books.

---

[3] In Greek mythology, Echo was a nymph who was condemned to speak only by repeating the last words spoken to her. She fell in love with Narcissus who rejected her and wasted away until her bones turned into stone. Only the sound of her voice as an echo remained.

Kosztolányi, D. (2011). The kleptomaniac translator. In D. Kosztolányi, *Kornél Esti* (B. Adams, Trans., pp. 199-203). New Directions Books.

Marías, J. (2000). *A heart so white*. (M. Jull-Costa, Trans.) New York: New Directions.

Marani, D. (2011). *New Finnish grammar* (J. Landry, Trans.). Dedalus. (Original work published 2000).

Marani. D. (2012) *The last of the Vostyachs* (J. Landry, Trans.). Dedalus. (Original work published 2002).

Marani, D. (2015). *The interpreter* (J. Landry, Trans.). Text Publishing. (Original work published 2004).

Miletich, M. (2018). Dragomans gaining footing: Translators as usurpers in two stories by Rodolfo Walsh and Moacyr Scliar. *Hikma, 17*, 175-195.

Pagano, A. S. (2002). Translation as testimony: On official stories and subversive pedagogies in Cortázar. In M. Tymoczco, & E. Gentzler (Eds.), *Translation and power* (pp. 80-98). University of Massachusetts Press.

Pirandello, L. (1922). *Six characters in search of an author*. (E. Storer, Trans.) E. P. Dutton.

Seneca. (2004). Letter LXVII. In *Letters from a stoic: Epistolae morales ad Lucilium* (R. Campbell, Trans., pp. 124-130). Penguin Books.

Spitzl, K. (2014). Fiction as a catalyst: Some afterthoughts. In K. Kaindl, & Karlheinz Spitzl (Eds.), *Transfiction: Research into the realities of translation fiction* (pp. 363-368). John Benjamins Publishing Company.

Steiner, G. (1998). *After babel: Aspects of language and translation*. New York: Oxford.

Vieira, E. R. (1995). (In)visibilidades na tradução: Troca de olhares teóricos e ficcionais. *Com Textos*(6), 50-68.

Walsh, R. (1981). La aventura de las pruebas de imprenta. In *Rodolfo Walsh: Obra literaria completa* (pp. 11-69). Siglo xxi editores.

Wilson, B. (1990). *Gaudí afternoon*. Seattle: The Seal Press.

Wilson, R. (2007) The fiction of the translator. *Journal of Intercultural Studies, 28*(4), 381-395.

Woodsworth, J. (Ed.). (2018). *The fictions of translation*. Amsterdam/Philadelphia: John Benjamins Publishing Company.

Yoshimoto, B. (1994). *NP.* (A. Sherif, Trans.) Faber & Faber.

Zunshine, L. (2006). *Why we read fiction: Theory of mind and the novel*. The Ohio State University Press.

Chapter 1

Diego Marani's Interpreters, Linguists, Lawbreakers and Loonies

Marella Feltrin-Morris

Ithaca College

Abstract: When featured at all, translators and interpreters tend to be employed in fictional works not so much for what they do or for any unique personality traits they may have as for what their occupation tends stereotypically to represent: an obsession with words, a frustration at being considered second-best to an idealized original, and a rarely-resisted temptation to take over the latter and finally enjoy the spotlight. Consequently, they often turn out to be flat characters, but contemporary literature is increasingly introducing more complex versions of these language professionals. Three novels by Diego Marani, *New Finnish Grammar* (2011), *The Last of the Vostyachs* (2012) and *The Interpreter* (2015),[1] portray interpreters, translators and linguists unleashing their fixations in curiously destructive manners. A close reading of these works examines how Marani engages with these clichés and what his take on them reveals in terms of faith or distrust in Language as a whole.

Keywords: interpreters, linguists, Marani, translation, Ursprache

***

Introduction

It is undeniable that translation and interpreting have increasingly acquired greater visibility, both as professions and as intellectual endeavors that deserve to be examined in their complexity, not dismissed as mere training to prepare for worthier creative feats. Still, the fictional character of the

---

[1] In the original Italian: *Nuova grammatica finlandese* (2000), *L'ultimo dei Vostiachi* (2002) and *L'interprete* (2004).

interpreter, and even more so of the translator, has yet to be utilized to its full potential. To some extent, this is quite understandable, especially with regards to translators: the day-to-day existence of someone pictured as mostly sitting at a desk and consulting dictionaries and thesauri can hardly be said to drive any suspenseful action or to deserve a baroque description. Fictional interpreters offer a broader range of opportunities—at least, they are mobile and can plausibly be catapulted into more perilous and exciting situations. Both, however, tend to be featured (when they are featured at all) not so much for what they do as for what their occupation tends stereotypically to represent, and therefore they turn out to be, more often than not, flat characters: reclusive, occasionally brilliant but almost invariably introverted, neurotic, living in the shadow of whatever author or interpreting organization they work for, and always on the verge of—or fully engaged in—doing something they should not be doing, which typically means overstepping their boundaries, forgetting their vow of neutrality and aspiring to take center stage when instead they are supposed to remain in the wings.

Nevertheless, perusing the shelves of modern and contemporary Italian literature, we discover several interesting figures, for example the diabolical Ermes Marana in Italo Calvino's 1979 novel, *If on a Winter's Night a Traveler*—a character who translates, transforms, manipulates and creates, loyal to none except to his theory that "literature's worth lies in its power of mystification, in mystification it has its truth; therefore a fake, as the mystification of a mystification, is tantamount to a truth squared" (Calvino, p. 180). Continuing our search, we find the protagonist of Francesca Duranti's *The House on Moon Lake* (1984), a translator bewitched by the book he discovered and translated to the point that he creates the muse that inspired it and succumbs to her. For an ethical take on translation, the hero of Antonio Tabucchi's 1994 novel *Pereira Maintains* is a journalist who also works as a translator in the Portugal of the 1930s and who decides to translate writers whose politics are in opposition to the dictatorial regime in which he lives. In this way, his translation journey signals the emergence of his social awareness.

It is during this quest for fictional translators and interpreters that we stumble upon a trio of novels published in the early 2000s: *New Finnish Grammar, The Last of the Vostyachs* and *The Interpreter*. The author, Diego Marani, is himself a former translator and revisor for the EU Council and, since 2015, Policy Coordinator for Cultural Diplomacy at the European External Action Service (EEAS). A frequent theme in Marani's books, as already evident from at least two of the titles, is language—language as an object of study, language as creation and language as an obsession. Marani is also the author of a pithy and informative essay, *Come ho imparato le lingue* ["How I Learned Foreign Languages"], and the creator of a constructed language, Europanto, a mixture of various languages reminiscent of Esperanto, but with a playful goal—indeed Marani writes, in this macaronic language, "Europanto want nicht informe aber amuse").[2] An examination of these three novels, where interpreters, translators and linguists unleash their fixations in curiously destructive ways, may shed some light on the extent to which a writer like Marani seeks to perpetuate, revisit, or debunk recurring representations of these professions and what these choices signify in terms of faith or distrust in Language as a whole.

New Finnish Grammar: Implanting a mother tongue

Although the first of the three novels does not directly deal with translation, it does inaugurate a language-related leitmotif that will be carried on in the other two, something that may actually be read as a catastrophic form of (self)-translation. Framed as the discovery, by the neurologist Petri Friari, of a manuscript written during WWII by a soldier Dr. Friari had treated for amnesia and wrongly identified as a Finn like himself, it tells the painful story of a man not only deprived of his past, but forced (albeit in good faith) to recover it by re-learning his mother tongue, only to find out that his attributed identity was itself a fabrication.

Instinctively drawn towards the badly-wounded soldier after seeing his name sewn into the inside of his collar, "Sampo Karjalainen," Dr. Friari—a Finnish exile in Germany—tends to him with almost fatherly care, seeing in him his younger self and determined to reunite him with his Finnish identity and with the country he himself sorely misses. Encouraged by Sampo's receptiveness to the first rudimentary Finnish lessons, Dr. Friari attributes the success of his re-education therapy to his hypothesis that, in Sampo's own words, "my brain cells had tracked down the remnants of my language which lay scattered among the folds of my wound" (Marani, 2011, p. 25).[3] The doctor makes plans for Sampo to be repatriated to Finland and urges him to work hard at recovering his Finnish mother tongue: "Finnish is the language in which you were brought up, the language of the lullaby that sent you to sleep each night. Apart from studying it, you must learn to love it. Think of each word as though it were a magic charm which might open the door to memory" (pp. 32-33). Once there, Sampo makes an earnest effort to find himself in the language, the people, the culture he supposedly comes from, but time and time again, he feels rejected and lonely. Even his friendship with the unconventional Pastor Koskela, who introduces him to the intricacies of

---

[2] D. Marani, "De Europanto Bricopolitik: Europantodag." http://www.europanto.be/eu ro7.html#350 (Last access 10/9/22)

[3] Hereafter cited by page number only.

Finnish syntax, vocabulary and lore, and with Ilma, a nurse whose love could heal him by making him turn outward to the future instead of inward where he is plagued by the absence of memories, proves ineffective. The final straw is his sighting of a warship whose name, "Sampo Karjalainen," reveals to him that all this time he had been pursuing a stranger, a ghost: "The identity I had built up for myself with so much difficulty crumbled away in an instant, was blown sky-high by that explosion of white letters rising from the sea like a shout, an insult, a jeer" (pp. 177-178). In utter despair, he clutches his pseudo-identity like a suicide weapon and goes off to the battlefield,[4] where he will find his death only a few days before Dr. Friari discovers the true identity of the man he had involuntarily turned into Sampo Karjalainen: his real name was Massimiliano Brodar, an Italian soldier who had been attacked by Stefan Klein, a German spy. Klein had stolen his uniform and dressed him in his own clothes, including his sailor jacket bearing the name of the ship "Sampo Karjalainen," where Klein had been working as a military instructor.

The story can be interpreted as an attempt at recovering an "original" text, i.e., Sampo's identity, which had been silenced. What Dr. Friari and then Pastor Koskela fail to realize is that the original text is one of their own creation, based upon their own traumas, fears, and desires. As "trans-lators," that is, as the individuals (self)-charged with carrying the "text" back to its roots, they unwittingly implant another essence into it, which does not represent it but which can no longer be cast off. Recognizing the risk of such a strategy, Pastor Koskela explains:

> Like so many glass vessels, forms contain the liquid that is words, which otherwise would seep away, dissolving into silence. The forms of a language inevitably have repercussions upon the speaker, it is they which mold his face, his land, his habits, where he lives, what he eats. (p. 53)

The reference to a vessel harkens back to Walter Benjamin's 1923 essay, "The Task of the Translator," and specifically to Benjamin's idea of the original and the translation being "recognizable as fragments of a greater language, just as fragments are part of a vessel" (Benjamin, 1968, p. 78).[5] When Koskela reassures Sampo by saying:

---

[4] Mirroring Pastor Koskela's own self-destruction.

[5] In setting up this analogy, Benjamin observes that "fragments of a vessel which are to be glued together must match one another in the smallest details, although they need not be like one another" (Benjamin, 1968, p. 78). In so doing, Benjamin moves beyond an idea of fidelity based solely on similarity, and points instead to a form of fidelity that is almost synonymous with spiritual devotion and with the recognition that every translation strives to achieve unity with the primordial Word.

If you were once Finnish, at some point or other you will find all this within you, because all this is not stored in your memory, it cannot be mislaid. It is in your blood, your guts. We are what remains of something extremely ancient, something which is bigger than ourselves and not of this world, (p. 54)

Is it faith in the existence of a higher entity, be it God or Language,[6] or is it precisely Koskela's bad faith, his cynicism, that leads to his and Sampo's demise?

As for Dr. Friari, his reconstruction of Sampo's identity through language smacks of mystification from the very beginning: Sampo's manuscript, by Dr. Friari's own admission, is "written in a spare, indeed broken and often ungrammatical Finnish" (p. 9), comes off as hardly convincing in the graceful and eloquent prose of Dr. Friari's rewriting. But if Sampo's manuscript ends up functioning not so much as a vehicle for Sampo to reclaim himself as a way for Dr. Friari to exorcize his own demons and, in his words, "to reconstruct my own story, my own identity, through other eyes" (p. 10), the ultimate irony might be that Marani's novel, written in Italian, provides the missing link between the forgotten Massimiliano Brodar and his lost identity.

The Last of the Vostyachs: The ethics of language preservation

Both in *New Finnish Grammar* and in *The Last of the Vostyachs*, Marani examines the indissoluble, yet problematic, relationship between language and identity. If, in the earlier book, he had portrayed a failed experiment in restoring one's identity through the imposition of a supposed mother tongue, in the 2002 novel, he focuses on the dark side of language preservation. How ethical, the reader is invited to ponder, is the effort of linguists to pry into the mystery of a dying language, to uproot it and *translate*[7] it for merely scientific purposes, or just to be declared the winner in a sterile rhetorical debate on linguistic ethnography?

The novel opens as Ivan, a Siberian native, experiences the first taste of freedom after spending most of his youth in a Russian gulag, where he and his father were imprisoned on the accusation of poaching and where he witnessed the brutal killing of his father, a traumatic event that had caused young Ivan to stop speaking. For the next twenty years, he "had not uttered a word" (Marani, 2012, p. 14).[8] When free at last, he returns to his native land, there is no one left to greet him. His people are all gone, "buried beneath the

---

[6] Not by chance, in one of his lessons, Pastor Koskela tells Sampo that "in Finnish, the word for Bible is *Raamattu*, that is, Grammar" (p. 125).

[7] In its etymological sense of carrying across.

[8] Hereafter cited by page number only.

black earth where moss and mushrooms grew. They had dissolved into the rotting mud that lay at the bottom of the pools, into the dark flesh of the berries, into the sickly sap of the birch trees, swayed by mysterious gusts of wind" (pp. 16-17). His language, too, is on the verge of extinction: as Olga Pavlovna, a Russian glottologist specializing in Uralic dialects, discovers on one of her field trips, he is the last speaker of Vostyach, a language[9] whose characteristics may "mark the transition between the Finnic languages and the Eskimo-Aleut ones," effectively disproving the uniqueness—hence the purity—of the Finno-Ugric languages and revealing instead that "languages belonging to the same family were spoken from the Baltic to the great plains of North America" (p. 31).

Enter Olga's counterpart: Jarmo Aurtova, an ambitious, ruthless linguistics professor and philanderer in his spare time, whose nationalist tendencies make him stop at nothing in order to uphold the absolute superiority of the Finnish language over all others. Out of nostalgia for the camaraderie of the good old days (Olga and Jarmo had been fellow students at university), Olga makes the unwise decision of enlisting Jarmo's help in welcoming Ivan to Helsinki, where she plans on showcasing him as the living proof of her sensational discovery at the 21st Conference of Finno-Ugric Languages. Predictably, Jarmo sets out to do just the opposite, i.e., eliminate every trace of the Vostyach's existence and preserve the primacy of Finnish. Caught between these two opposing forces, Ivan comes off as an inconvenient "text" to be translated: should he, like a noble savage, be *domesticated*[10] and his language stripped of its mysteries and categorized, his vocabulary and metaphors rendered through equivalent, familiar expressions? Or should he be *foreignized*—treated as the perennial Other, displayed as an exotic specimen to highlight how he is, untranslatable, although well translatable, into a possible promotion for the researcher who discovered him? Jarmo has a third, diabolical plan: that of silencing him altogether and then dispensing with Olga, his potential "translator," whom he lures into his summer cottage, renders unconscious by spiking her drink, and dumps in a deserted beach where she will freeze to death. But even after Olga has been successfully disposed of, Ivan has, unbeknownst to Jarmo, broken free of the supervision of a boorish Laplander who, according to the professor's orders, was supposed to get the last of the Vostyachs "good and drunk" and ship him off to Sweden (p. 51). The suddenly unbridled Ivan goes on to cause havoc throughout the

---

[9] While Nganasan, the Samoyedic language to which it is compared, actually exists, Vostyach is an invention of Marani's.

[10] To use Lawrence Venuti's renowned dichotomy, domestication vs. foreignization. See Venuti, *The Translator's Invisibility: A History of Translation* (1995).

algid Finnish capital, accompanied by a menagerie of animals he liberated from the zoo.

The novel itself strikes the reader as a mishmash of irreconcilable genres and cinematic influences: the treatment of the noble savage theme appears heavily indebted to Akira Kurosawa's 1975 film *Dersu Uzala,*[11] but some scenes also call to mind Levy's *Night at the Museum* while others could fit well in a splatter movie, and the satire on academic life is not unlike what one would find in a David Lodge novel.[12] It is, however, the substantial sections devoted to the lifespan and death of languages and to those who, for egotistic or philanthropic purposes, seek to preserve them that come off as most sincere. A recurring question and the core of the diatribe between Jarmo and Olga is whether a language is better off by being left alone, revered in its superior isolation, immutable and "permanently frozen, like the arctic ice" (p. 107) or whether it has a better chance of survival by being dissected and studied with scientific curiosity,[13] or disseminated, absorbed and *translated.* The two linguists, their tongues even looser after imbibing generous amounts of alcohol, pull no punches in attacking each other's native language (Finnish and Russian, respectively) as being the supreme example of either of those tendencies. "Perhaps that is why we've managed to stand up to you," argues Jarmo, "why we have never been drowned out by the Slavic tide: by using our sounds sparingly, transmitting them intact from generation to generation, honed by use" (pp. 107-108). "Your language has never known the dizzying heights of universality," Olga snaps back. "No one studies it, and all you can do is to repeat it among yourselves because it tells of a tiny country no one knows" (p. 108). While it is clear that both, in their intoxicated vehemence, are making sweeping, unsubstantiated statements, their contrasting positions on the benefits and detriments of translation are quite thought-provoking: "Our language is translated into a hundred others," says Olga. "A hundred other peoples want to understand us and invent words in their own language which express our truths" (p. 108). But if Olga praises translation for enriching the

---

[11] Based on a memoir by the Russian explorer Vladimir Arsenyev, Kurosawa's *Dersu Uzala* centers around a nomadic trapper in the Russian Far East.

[12] Known for his bitingly humorous take on academia, David Lodge is particularly famous for the campus trilogy, *Changing Places: A Tale of Two Campuses* (1975), *Small World: An Academic Romance* (1984) and *Nice Work* (1988).

[13] Despite being a practitioner of this method, Olga questions her own motives when she admits: "I asked myself if we are indeed really salvaging something when we preserve these now vanished languages in formalin like so many freakish animals. Are we not in fact rather pandering to some personal obsession of our own, of no more use to anyone else than a collection of beer mats or cigarette packets?" (p. 37).

target language and rendering it more equipped to express hitherto unfathomable concepts, Jarmo despises it for the very same reason:

> Translation causes a language to become soiled; like blood in a transfusion, which is gradually tainted by impurities. Your language is a phial of blood on a hospital shelf, a curdled mass of random droppings. Ours on the other hand is a young vein, full of life, the fruit of a single body. By being translated, a language picks up meanings which are not its own, which infect it and poison it, and against which it has no defenses. It is like the native Americans, who were wiped out by European diseases. Today they are almost all dead, their languages so many unpronounceable relics, tangled heaps of sound which no alphabet could ever unpick. (pp. 108-109)

As the undisputed villain among all the characters, Jarmo has jurisdiction over almost every white supremacist statement in the novel, towards which the reader is expected (required, even?) to react with superior outrage. The notion that translation brings about, as one of its noxious side effects, a poisoning of the target language sounds like a sinister re-reading of the famous 1816 essay "Upon the Proper Manner and Usefulness of Translations," where Madame De Staël argued:

> although one should have a very sufficient knowledge of foreign languages, when he takes up a good translation of a foreign poet into his own tongue, he will receive a pleasure yet more intimate and domestic than any which he has previously received from these writings, in the contemplation of those new colors and ornaments which his vernacular tongue is receiving, from the *appropriation* of beauties to which it had in former times been a stranger. (1817, p. 145, my emphasis)[14]

To be fair, even De Staël's position, despite the gentle evocation of "colors" and "ornaments," refers to the process that precedes and induces such enrichment of the target language more crudely as one of "appropriation." Or does it? In reality, De Staël makes no mention of appropriation in her original French manuscript, which was solicited by an Italian journal, *La Biblioteca Italiana*, and where it was first published in translation. That is where the

---

[14] Similarly to Madame De Staël, the German Romantics such as Friedrich Schlegel and Wilhelm von Humboldt regarded translation as a means by which to expand the potential of the target language. An overview of their positions can be found in Antoine Berman's *The Experience of the Foreign: Culture and Translation in Romantic Germany* (1992).

word *appropriandosi* first appears, and the English translation, based upon the Italian, maintains the forceful imagery. If this detour through the Italian and English incarnations of De Staël's essay may seem to lose sight of Marani's provocation as uttered by Jarmo, it intends to emphasize the complexity of the representation of translation as an act of violence. The victim of such violence is usually identified as the language/culture being appropriated and colonized. In "The Hermeneutic Motion," George Steiner develops the metaphor of violence quite extensively, drawing a connection with Jerome and with the image, evoked by the latter, of "meaning brought home captive by the translator" and associating comprehension with the breaking of a code: "decipherment is dissective, leaving the shell smashed and the vital layers stripped" (2004, p. 194).[15] And the imperialistic mission of "dominating the vernacular" is also explored in depth in Vicente Rafael's *Contracting Colonialism* (1993, p. 26). Yet, appropriation can go both ways. In his nationalistic paranoia, Jarmo fears the power of the vernacular to insinuate itself under the skin of the presumably "pure," dominant language, contaminating it with its sounds, syntax, symbols, and values and, perhaps, as the final blow, even revealing itself to have engendered them in the first place.

But what about the "naïve" Ivan? His language is described as being seamlessly connected to the sounds of nature, to the point that, when he first regains use of it after over two decades of silence, "all nature quaked. Things that had not been named for years emerged sluggishly from their long sleep, realizing they still existed" (pp. 15-16). When he sings, his voice is "majestic," shamanic, and needs to be held in check, "as though it might unleash something uncontrollable, superhuman" (p. 36). The organic quality of his language, along with the ostensible innocence of his character, places him in stark contrast to the "civilized" Jarmo, who is portrayed in such a consistently negative light as to overshadow any vicious or even barbarous acts committed by others. As a result, the reader seems encouraged to turn a blind eye on the fact that even Ivan, at once terrified and aroused when forced into a sexual encounter with a prostitute who will supposedly keep him occupied until he is put on a ship to Sweden, ends up brutally raping the girl and unintentionally killing her. Is this reaction supposed to be interpreted as a warning against the manipulative domestication of the Other? Or has the Other been foreignized to such an extent that he can only be expected to behave like a wild beast?

The novel's denouement is also quite ambiguous but intriguing at the same time: following Olga's death and Jarmo's imprisonment, the arcane Vostyach

---

[15] Steiner argues that "the translator invades, extracts, and brings home" (Steiner, 2004, p. 194).

language remains inaccessible to all, and yet within everyone's reach: as an improbable entertainer and modern-day Pied Piper,

> on a cruise ship plying the Baltic from Helsinki to Stockholm, the last of the Vostyachs earns his living by performing with the Estonian folk group 'Neli Sardelli.' He plays a drum made of reindeer skin, singing the ancient songs of a mysterious language which makes your hair stand up on end; which makes you want to pray. (p. 166)

Untranslated and ungraspable, the prodigious vernacular will still not be silenced: disguised as a raucous distraction, it makes its way into even the most recalcitrant languages, transforming them from within:

> Slowly, the people around him started repeating the odd word, then a verse, then the whole song. In the freezing night, the whole Baltic echoed with the song of the men of the tundra which had come down from the distant peaks of the Byrranga Mountains to the land of the thousand lakes. (p. 150)

The Interpreter: A quest for the primordial language

Language as obsession is at the core of the novel *The Interpreter*—the one, among the three, that makes the most of the metaphorical potential of its central character, who also gives the novel its title. The interpreter's quest for a protolanguage, an *Ursprache*, again calls to mind Benjamin's "The Task of the Translator."[16] What emerges as particularly interesting is the almost shamanic role of Marani's interpreter, who possesses, partly as an innate quality and partly as what in Italian is called *deformazione professionale* (a quirk developed as a result of one's job), the unique capacity to communicate with the non-human universe, to intercept, that is, the non-verbal language of nature.

The plot is rather complex and justifies the words in the blurb, which call the book "both a quest and a thriller, and at times a comic picaresque caper around Europe, but [that] also deals with the profound issues of existence." In the very beginning, the narrator informs the reader:

> This is the story of my undoing: of how one single man snatched me from those I loved, from my profession, from my private life, and bore

---

[16] As Benjamin famously argues, "it is the task of the translator to release in his own language that pure language which is under the spell of another, to liberate the language imprisoned in a work in his re-creation of that work" (Benjamin, 1968, p. 80).

me to my ruin, a prey to confusion and mind-befogging illness. Not that this was his callous aim: he couldn't help himself." (Marani, 2015, p. 9)[17]

One soon learns that the man being referred to is the interpreter, whom Félix Bellamy, the narrator and director of the interpreters' department of a prestigious international institution, was forced to suspend because of his employee's outlandish behavior. As the Report received by Bellamy reads,

> Mr. XXX,[18] while engaged in his work as a simultaneous interpreter, emits completely meaningless sounds and whistles; he translates inattentively, adding words of his own invention, which do not figure in the speaker's speech; he indulges in long pauses,interrupting the translation, and expresses himself in languages other than those required for the meeting in question. (p. 17)

When he is summoned to a meeting and questioned about his behavior, the interpreter vehemently protests that what he is producing are not meaningless sounds but a new, or perhaps ancient language, which has mysteriously infiltrated his mind and become entangled with the other fifteen languages he knows, and it is now his duty to disentangle it and make it available to the rest of the world. It is the language of the universe, proclaims the interpreter almost in a frenzy, "the one concealed in the eternal polar ice, the one lurking in the chasms of the oceans, the one which has commanded matter since the dawn of time!" (p. 31). Convinced that the man is deranged, Bellamy does not give in to his plea to be allowed to continue his work as a simultaneous interpreter, keeps chasing after the language of the universe, and suspends him on the grounds of disability. However, this decision comes back to haunt him since soon he finds himself afflicted by the same ailment and emits unintelligible, non-human sounds. And so he, too, embarks in an obsessive quest, not for the language but for a cure against this extreme form of polyglotism, which leads him first to Munich, to the specialist who had first diagnosed the illness that had struck the interpreter (who in the meantime has disappeared), where he undergoes a bizarre detoxifying language cure, and from there to Odessa, Klaipeda (Lithuania) and Tallinn, following an arcane geographic itinerary that he found in the interpreter's apartment. The quest itself, just like Bellamy's language, personality, and even his identity, becomes progressively more confused, and the book, which initially read like a psychological thriller, now starts resembling a Gothic novel interspersed with some chases that would be suitable for a spy story, as well as with some

---

[17] Hereafter cited by page number only.
[18] The interpreter remains nameless throughout the novel.

echoes of Pirandello's *The Late Mattia Pascal*[19] and *One, No One and One Hundred Thousand.* The story ends at the Tallinn Aquarium, where, at last, Bellamy reunites with the interpreter, who announces to him triumphantly that he found the mysterious language to which he had fallen prey: it is, he says, "the language of when we were fish, dark scaly inhabitants of the ocean's depths, and God didn't even know he had created us" (p. 211). In other words, the interpreter can communicate in the dolphin language, while Bellamy was fooled, as he had been deviously inoculated with the rare language of the southern Tursiops, a dolphin subspecies, and remains an outcast even among them like a tragic, failed experiment.

What stands out in Marani's book is not so much the figure of the translator or interpreter as a somewhat freakish juggler of words, a victim of inexplicable phenomena,[20] nor is it surprising to see him depicted as a trickster, a manipulator of messages, a betrayer of meaning, since those, too, are rather common clichés of these professional categories. What is more thought-provoking, rather, is the insistence on the interpreter's attachment not to a specific text as to language, and not a specific language, but the primordial language, the *Ursprache*—actually, a language even older than the *Ursprache*, a language that precedes humanity itself.[21] This characteristic is not even an exclusive attribute of the interpreter being hunted by Bellamy, but of all interpreters, whom the narrator compares from the very beginning to animals:

> In the canteen, in the bar, in the local restaurants, in the entrance halls of our various offices, they formed groups of wildly gesticulating, wild-eyed individuals, endlessly prattling, leaping from one language to another like acrobats, sometimes prone to fitful movements, reminiscent of those made for no apparent reason by a fish or bird.

Before disappearing and thus motivating the desperate chase that occupies most of the novel, the interpreter materializes before Bellamy, looking almost bird-like, his face grotesquely deformed in the effort of emitting non-human sounds. And yet, in spite of this privileged connection to nature, the primeval universe to which the interpreter has access does not seem to reveal anything except an insurmountable distance and the indifference of the cosmos for the destiny of man. If the task of the translator is, as Benjamin argues, that of producing in the target language "an echo of the original" (1968, p. 76), what

---

[19] At a certain point Bellamy even takes on a fake name.
[20] Marani's limits himself to emitting whistles and squeals, but the translator in Julio Cortázar's "Letter to a Young Lady in Paris" goes as far as to vomit bunny rabbits.
[21] This is of course another nod to Benjamin.

echo can Marani's interpreter possibly capture and offer? Only the echo of silence, of absence. The negation of that which justifies his function. Significantly, the novel ends with an appeal to that absent creator:

> Quite recently, I have begun to pray [...] All I am asking is to understand... But looking at the crucifix on the altar, there in the silence of that lonely little wooden church, I am suddenly struck by the awful feeling that it is I who am a mistake, that all humanity is just an accident; that God himself is a dolphin, up there in his heaven, whistling mockingly at my prayers, flapping his fins and waving his snout in the celestial heights of a watery paradise. (p. 217)

The devotion to a God forever separated from man by a linguistic abyss seems to hit at the heart of the modern interpreter's tragedy: if, in the past, Dante Alighieri (among others) had denounced the incapacity of translation to reproduce the sweetness of the original (2002, p. 48), for Marani's interpreter who moves backward from language to language through the history of mankind, translation represents the frantic pursuit of an original message that might not exist and that, even if it did exist, would not be communicable anyway. Therefore, the impulse that drives the interpreter—and all interpreters—is not the effort to make some meaning intelligible, to reproduce it faithfully by trans-lating it, i.e., by carrying it across (the barriers of language, space, and time), but it is the very quest for meaning, the irrational hope that, in the course of this journey, some fragment of meaning, like a leaf or a grain of sand, might stubbornly cling to him, and in so doing testify to at least the possibility of a higher order and of reciprocal understanding. In this light, interpreters emerge like fragile modern heroes.

And speaking of journeys, it is certainly not by chance that the narrator, at the end of the novel, announces that he made a virtue out of necessity and, in the impossibility of going home to a land where he would find himself irremediably alone, he learned Estonian and became, despite himself, an interpreter, specifically one who shows "parties of schoolchildren and tourists around the dolphinarium" (p. 216).

Conclusion

One might be tempted to conclude that interpreters have a thankless profession. Not one freely chosen but imposed by some chameleonic anomaly of the personality, which forces these wretched individuals to embark on some sort of pilgrimage in search of an impossible truth, soaking oneself in a linguistic bath that may cleanse or kill them. To those who uphold, first of all, the ethical value of translation and its mission—that is, to create bridges between cultures by bringing individuals and societies together under a shared faith in the possibility of communication and in the power of the word, this portrait comes off as narcissistic and defeatist, or in the very least limited. And if injecting a certain dose of narcissism into the representation of a craft or art still considered servile or invisible can actually be beneficial, one is still left perplexed by the numerous warnings against polyglotism, one of which is reprinted on the back cover of the Italian edition of the book: "Languages are like toothbrushes: the only one you should put in your mouth is your own. It's a question of hygiene, of good manners" (Marani, 2015, p. 15).[22] Soon after that consideration, the narrator goes as far as to compare languages to evil germs that carry mysterious illnesses: "a foreign language injected into our mind brings with it the taint of unknown sounds, a vision of worlds that are incomprehensible to us—the lure of other truths and a devilish desire to know them" (Marani, 2015, pp. 15-16).[23]

But how can this be anything except a provocation by the narrator and by Marani himself, both of them bewitched by the magic of languages and by the evocative power of the word, especially if foreign? In *The Interpreter*, but also in the powerfully lyrical *New Finnish Grammar* and in the dark, haunting *The Last of the Vostyachs*, language obsesses, cures, destroys, charms, molds the personality but at the same time makes it unstable; the only constant element is, indeed, the passion, sometimes desperate, other times amused (as we see in Marani's essay, *Come ho imparato le lingue*) for this elusive allurer. Lastly, the narrator, Félix Bellamy, is a French-speaking Swiss; therefore, the novel itself, written in Italian, turns out to be a translation, and thus yet another veiled homage to an art that, for a change, is not represented in terms of compliance, competition, or rebellion against an original, but as a shared, assiduous respect for the secular, but no less sacred, Word.

---

[22] Similarly, only minutes before being arrested for murder, Prof. Jarmo Aurtova in *The Last of the Vostyachs* had given a fanatic speech advocating for monolingualism, declaring that "only ignorance can protect us from extinction" and exhorting his countrymen not to "study the language of the foreigner, but force him to learn your own!" (Marani, 2012, p. 155).

[23] The same idea had also been expressed by Dr. Friari in *New Finnish Grammar*: "A learnt language is just a mask, a form of borrowed identity; it should be approached with appropriate aloofness, and its speaker should never yield to the lure of mimicry, renouncing the sounds of his own language to imitate those of another. Anyone who gives in to this temptation is in danger of losing their memory, their past, without receiving another in exchange" (Marani, 2011, p. 52).

References

Alighieri, D. (2002). "Translation destroys the sweetness of the original" (K. Hillard, Trans.). In *Western translation theory: From Herodotus to Nietzsche*, ed. D. Robinson, St. Jerome Publishing, pp. 47-48.

Benjamin, W. (1968). The task of the translator. *Illuminations* (H. Zohn, Trans.). Schocken Books, pp. 69-82. (Original work published 1923).

Berman, A. (1992). *The experience of the foreign: Culture and translation in romantic Germany* (S. Heyvaert, Trans.). SUNY Press. (Original work published 1984).

Calvino, I. (1981). *If on a winter's night a traveler* (W. Weaver, Trans.). Harcourt Brace & Company. (Original work published 1979).

Cortázar, J. (1967). Letter to a young lady in Paris. In *Blow-Up and other stories* (P. Blackburn, Trans.). Pantheon Books. (Original work published 1951).

Duranti, F. (1986). *The house on moon lake* (S. Sartarelli, Trans.). Random House. (Original work published 1984).

Jerome (1997). The best kind of translator (P. Carroll, Trans.). In *Western translation theory: From Herodotus to Nietzsche*, ed. D. Robinson, St. Jerome Publishing, pp. 22-30.

Kurosawa, A. (Director). (1975). *Dersu Uzala*. [Film]. Daiei Film.

Levy, S. (Director). (2006). *Night at the museum*. [Film]. 20th Century Studios.

Lodge, D. (1975). *Changing places: A tale of two campuses*. Secker & Warburg.

Lodge, D. (1984). *Small world: An academic romance*. Secker & Warburg.

Lodge, D. (1988). *Nice work*. Secker & Warburg.

Marani, D. (2005). *Come ho imparato le lingue* ["How I Learned Foreign Languages"]. passSaggi Bompiani.

Marani, D. (2011). *New Finnish grammar* (J. Landry, Trans.). Dedalus. (Original work published 2000).

Marani. D. (2012) *The last of the Vostyachs* (J. Landry, Trans.). Dedalus. (Original work published 2002).

Marani, D. (2015). *The interpreter* (J. Landry, Trans.). Text Publishing. (Original work published 2004).

Marani, D. (n.d.) De Europanto Bricopolitik: Europantodag. http://www.euro panto.be/euro7.html#350 (Last access 10/9/22)

Pirandello, L. (1966). *The late Mattia Pascal* (W. Weaver, Trans.). Anchor Books. (Original work published 1904).

Pirandello, L. (1992). *One, no one, and one hundred thousand* (W. Weaver, Trans.). Marsilio Publishers. (Original work published 1926).

Rafael, V. (1993). *Contracting colonialism: Translation and Christian conversion in Tagalog society under early Spanish rule*. Duke University Press.

Staël, Madame de. (1817). Upon the proper manner and usefulness of translations. (n.t.). *Blackwood's Edinburgh Magazine 2*(8), 145-149. (Original work published 1816).

Steiner, G. (2004). The hermeneutic motion, In *The translation studies reader*, ed. L. Venuti. 2nd Edition. Routledge, pp. 193-98.

Tabucchi, A. (2010). *Pereira Maintains* (P. Creagh, Trans.). New Directions. (Original work published 1994).

Venuti, L. (1995) *The translator's invisibility: A history of translation.* Routledge.

Chapter 2

The Interpreter's Visibility and Agency in Yuri Herrera's *Signs Preceding the End of the World*[1]

Caragh Barry

University of California, Santa Barbara

Abstract: Fiction featuring interpreters has often included several tropes to describe these characters. Among these interpreter-characters as portrayed in fiction, perhaps the most (in)famous is La Malinche/Malintzin/Malinalli/Doña Marina. La Malinche has often been portrayed as either a self-interested, lustful traitor who interprets for her own personal gain at the expense of her community, as a victim of patriarchal and colonial circumstances with limited agency to help herself, let alone "her people," or she has been reevaluated as a feminist symbol. Yuri Herrera's 2009 novella *Signs Preceding the End of the World* uses a Malinche-esque character who, removed from the actual context of the conquest, is fully able to both engage with questions of individual interpreter agency and fulfillment as well as contest the negative interpretations of La Malinche's involvement. Ultimately, Herrera positively portrays the visibility of this modern Malinche and the agency she possesses as an interpreter in the face of great power imbalances, even when her actions seemingly go against the interpreter's own stated ethics.

Keywords: agency, La Malinche, translator/interpreter activism, translator/interpreter visibility, Herrera

***

---

[1] The text of this chapter is based on a section of the author's doctoral dissertation entitled *It's Always Personal: Exploring Translator/Interpreter Agency and Emotion through Translator/Interpreter Characters in Hispanic and Lusophone Fiction,* University of California, Santa Barbara, 2023.

Introduction

Like the representation of the translator in works of transfiction, the characterization of interpreters seems to also fall into certain categories that have since become tropes. Interpreter and scholar Ingrid Kurz neatly defines some of these common tropes in her 2007 article "The Fictional Interpreter" as well as in her 2014 chapter "On the (in)fidelity of (fictional) interpreters." In the latter, Kurz categorizes fictional interpreters based on their reasons for violating the commonly held expectation for translators and interpreters to remain faithful to the message they are imparting by not altering, embellishing, or omitting any portion of it. Among Kurz's categorizations, there are several tropes for interpreters that emerge, the most notable of which are the interpreter as "a kind of machine, that they translate automatically" (2007, p. 278), the interpreter as a sort of activist who either "betray[s] the client to prevent foul play" (2014, p. 207) or "side[s] with the underprivileged" (2014, p. 208), and the selfish and treacherous interpreter who manipulates the message for their own benefit (2014, pp. 211-212). These tropes are further explored by Karlheinz Spitzl in his "Taking care of the stars: Interpreted interaction in Amadou Hampâté Bâ's *L'étrange Destin De Wangrin*" (2014, pp.103-122) and Maria Todorova's "Interpreting conflict: Memories of an interpreter" (2014, pp. 221-231). Both scholars examine interpreter characters who are either selfish and interpreting only for themselves (in the case of Bâ's fictional interpreter) or who, despite trying to be an activist interpreter and helping to mitigate conflict, show an interpreter character who is viewed as suspect simply for associating themselves with the invading force (Todorova, 2014). Interestingly, these tropes for interpreter characters bring forward the question of the power and agency exercised in interpretation, along with the consequences and societal judgments based on exercising said power.

With the simple fact that no two languages or cultures are exactly alike, the translator or interpreter inevitably must make decisions in their process, and therefore, machine-like, total perfection and neutrality is impossible. Yet, in contrast to the translator, both in and outside of fiction, the interpreter inherently has a trickier sort of "power" and agency. Interpreters are inevitably visible due to their physical presence and immediate intervention in the act of linguistic transfer, and therefore, their involvement in the process is much more noticeable and, at times, more suspect. Given the struggle of these pressures and the complexities involved in interpreting, once it began to be recognized as a profession, numerous professional groups and guilds began to set forth codes of ethics and standards to help guide practitioners. However, even these codes were often contradictory. For example, a 1997 study found that when posed with hypothetical yet realistic situations in which an interpreter might be persuaded to act against their professional code of ethics to intervene or interject in a situation, many interpreters would do so based on their personal morals (Tate & Turner, 2002). Indeed, the researchers found that several interpreters were inclined to even serve as advocates for the people for whom they were interpreting (Tate & Turner, 2002, p. 380). Therefore, the researchers concluded that "...interpreters are looking for more fully articulated written guidelines and a more fully developed education in how to use the Code with sensitivity to context" (Tate & Turner, 2002, p. 382). In the almost thirty years since this study was published, professional codes of ethics and standards have been reevaluated with an eye to these varying contexts and advocacy. However, it is clear from just a few examples that the debate among the community of scholars and practicing interpreters on how to best approach these dilemmas of neutrality and non-involvement versus visibility and advocacy is far from resolved.

When it comes to exploring these debates via fiction, perhaps the most recognizable figure used to represent them is that of La Malinche/Malintzin/Malinalli/Doña Marina,[2] the indigenous woman who interpreted for Hernán Cortés during the sixteenth-century Spanish conquest and colonization of what is now modern-day Mexico. For her role in the conquest, Malinche has variously been maligned as a traitor, hailed as a hero, and pitied as a victim. To make matters more complex, the historical La Malinche never learned to read or write, nor did she leave any direct record of her thoughts or experiences as an interpreter. Consequently, history can never truly know her motivations or her feelings regarding her time with the Spaniards.

Amid this debate on the agency of La Malinche and how history should judge her involvement in the conquest enters Yuri Herrera's 2009 novella *Signs Preceding the End of the World*,[3] translated into English by Lisa Dillman and published by & Other Stories Press in 2015. This novella offers a unique perspective on the debates about agency regarding La Malinche and

---

[2] All four of these names have been used at various points throughout history to refer to the same woman. While Malintzin and Malinalli are the closest approximations to her indigenous name, Doña Marina is the name by which the Spaniards referred to her after her baptism. Throughout this chapter, however, she will be referred to as La Malinche for two reasons: one, because she is most widely known throughout history and in popular culture as "La Malinche," and two, because the use of this name encompasses the mythical and figurative connotations that the use of her figure as a symbol has garnered throughout the centuries. For a more detailed discussion on the evolution of the name(s) of this historical interpreter figure, please see Frances Karttunen's 1994 work *Between Worlds: Interpreters, Guides, and Survivors* (p. 6) and Pilar Godayol's 2012 "Malintzin/La Malinche/Doña Marina: Re-reading the myth of the treacherous translator."

[3] *Señales que precederán al fin del mundo*. All the quotes from the novel included within this chapter are taken directly from the published English translation.

community interpreters faced with similar power imbalances. By taking a Malinche-esque character without using the actual historical figure, the novella is able to separate the question of the "interpreter as traitor" from the baggage of La Malinche as a historical symbol, as "Mexican Eve," or as a cultural mother to give her back her agency. This reexamination of the interpreter's role embraces and accepts the biases and flaws inherent in the process of interpretation rather than attempting to hold the interpreter to an impossible standard of perfection and invisibility. Finally, the novella offers the reader a view of an interpreter-as-activist who finds fulfillment in her profession and does not need to stop interpreting in order to find her "own" voice. While this approach in *Signs* may not be appropriate for all (or even most) interpreting situations, it contrasts with prevailing representations of both La Malinche and interpreters as alternately powerless and invisible or powerful and traitorous.

La Malinche: History's most (in)famous interpreter

The sixteenth-century indigenous woman known most widely as La Malinche has garnered fame for her role as an interpreter and facilitator during one of the monumental first encounters between European and Native American cultures. Consequently, she has been mythologized and used as a symbol for a variety of agendas and national projects, with her image and figure appearing in numerous important documents concerning the conquest and foundations of present-day Mexico. From the *Florentine Codex* (de Sahagún et al.) and Bernal Díaz del Castillo's *True History of the Conquest of New Spain*[4] to murals and other more modern works of art featuring her together with Cortés, La Malinche has loomed large in the Mexican cultural imaginary for centuries. Yet despite this very literal visibility, like stereotypical good translators and interpreters whose presence must not be detected while they work, La Malinche was illiterate and therefore could not directly share her own thoughts on her life, thoughts, and lived experiences with history. Due to the lack of a first-person account, this left ample room for her figure to be used as fertile ground for debates on national identity, women's rights, and the role of interpreters, independently of what the actual historical figure may have believed or supported. Over the years, the historical La Malinche has received countless amounts of both praise and scorn for her actions during the conquest. In short, she has been variously hailed as the mythical mother of the Mexican and Chicanx people and pitied as a victim of rape, patriarchy, colonialism, and extremely unfortunate historical circumstances. For centuries La Malinche was decried as Cortés's whore and a treacherous traitor to her

---

[4] *Historia verdadera de la conquista de la Nueva España.*

"fellow natives."[5] In perhaps the most well-known work on La Malinche as a symbol, Octavio Paz (1949; translated into English in 1961) interpreted her as a victim of her historical circumstances in his essay "The Sons of La Malinche."[6] In the essay, Paz meditates on the nature and mythical origin story of the Mexican people. He suggests a violent, essentialist point of origin with the relationship between the conqueror Hernán Cortés and La Malinche. Paz alludes to La Malinche as "the *Chingada*"[7] and claims that she gave herself willingly to Cortés: "It is true that she gave herself voluntarily to the conquistador, but he forgot her as soon as her usefulness was over" (1961, p. 86). Much like the biblical Eve, whose curiosity and naiveté are blamed for man's downfall, La Malinche betrayed her "fellow natives" in favor of the Spanish conquerors. Paz (1961) suggests that by her very nature as a woman, she is passive and necessarily prone to violence, especially sexual violence. He writes, "Her taint is constitutional and resides, as we said earlier, in her sex. ...And yet she is the cruel incarnation of the feminine condition" (Paz, 1961, pp. 85-86). La Malinche is inherently a victim, but also a traitor.

In recent decades, a more compassionate approach to her legacy has been undertaken. She has even been respected for her skill and hailed as a hero for how she interpreted (Del Castillo, 1974), and La Malinche's native context has been reexamined and reinserted into the conversation, allowing for the fact that skilled native women like her were operating based on a complex web of needs, desires, historical context, and political goals (Jager, 2015, p. 5). In the cultural evaluation of her role, La Malinche has simultaneously been a traitor and a victim, a selfish individual interpreting for her own personal gain and incapable of exercising her agency and changing her or Mexico's fate. In short, her agency has been both accepted and denied: she alternatively has been seen as a figure with agency (by her will and ability to betray her "fellow" natives by giving into her sexual desires; by the ability to selectively translate Cortés's speech and mitigate worse outcomes of the conquest; and by the ability to have chosen not to serve as interpreter for the Spaniards) or a helpless victim of her circumstances (a sexual slave to Cortés and a prisoner

---

[5] This concept has been contested due to the fact that at the time she lived there was no concept of "indigenous people" as a collective, but rather there were multiple socio-cultural-political groups with a variety of different relationships among themselves. See Rebecca Jager's (2015) *Malinche, Pocahontas, and Sacagawea: Indian Women as Cultural Intermediaries and National Symbols* and Roberto Valdeón's (2013) "Doña Marina/La Malinche: A historiographical approach to the interpreter/traitor" for a more detailed discussion of this topic.

[6] "Los hijos de La Malinche."

[7] "The Fucked Woman"; my translation. The published English-language translation of Paz's essay leaves this term in the original Spanish.

in the brutal process of Spanish conquest). In other words, it is impossible to summarily categorize this woman and say that La Malinche was simply a victim of the patriarchal society in which she lived, merely a victim of colonial conquest, or, conversely, a staunch feminist actor who employed what agency she had to protect her "fellow natives" from harm or to become a selfish traitor.

In works of fiction, La Malinche's representation has fared about the same as her historical one, shifting accordingly with how her figure was employed as a symbol in the national conversation, a symbol onto which nationalist, religious, feminist, and even translation/interpretation ideology could be inscribed (Valdeón, 2013, p. 173). Focusing solely on La Malinche as a metaphor for translation (Godayol, 2012, pp. 70-74), as an interpreter, La Malinche exemplifies several stereotypical tropes applied to interpreters and translators alike as seen in fiction and in cultural discourse at large (i.e., the interpreter as a self-interested traitor, the interpreter as invisible or powerless, and the interpreter as "vessel" for the male author's text). As Sandra Messinger Cypess (1991) notes in *La Malinche in Mexican Literature: from History to Myth*: "from great lady to Terrible Mother, La Malinche serves the particular historical needs of a complex society in change," (p. 9). Several works in the twentieth and twenty-first centuries feature her as a character, and these works have reflected many of the opinions held about her in the culture at large. In "The Two Shores"[8] (1994; originally published in 1993) by Carlos Fuentes, La Malinche is portrayed as an untrustworthy seductress, falling in line with the trope of the interpreter as a selfish traitor. Fuentes's short story is told as if from beyond the grave from the perspective of Jerónimo de Aguilar, the shipwrecked clergy member who had been captured by the Maya and later served in the chain of interpreters for Cortés along with La Malinche. Aguilar shows La Malinche as a traitor, describing her intervening in order to benefit the Spaniards (and herself) while Aguilar intervenes to help the Aztecs (and also himself) (Fuentes, 1994, pp. 16-19). Fuentes's story also goes on to describe her as "...the treacherous woman from Tabasco" (p. 17) and "the diabolical female [...] this bitch of a Marina, this whore [...]. This scoundrel, this trickster, this expert in sucking, the conquistador's concubine," (Fuentes, p. 24). With the employment of this harsh, sexual, and misogynist language along with the statement that La Malinche is also the "mother and origin of a new nation, which perhaps could only be born and grow against the charges of abandonment, illegitimacy, and betrayal..." (Fuentes, p. 33), Fuentes's portrayal echoes the interpretation of La Malinche put forth by Paz. Here again, she is both traitor and victim, and these roles are inexorably tied to her

---

[8] "Las dos orillas." All quotes from this short story are taken from the published English translation.

identity as a woman, and as an interpreter, especially when he describes how La Malinche "...had pulled the Spanish language out of Cortés's sex, she'd sucked it out of him," (Fuentes, 1994, p. 25).

Conversely, feminist and Chicana writers have for decades now been contesting this claim of La Malinche as a victim and traitor, and instead have chosen to emphasize her role as a cultural mother. In doing so, these writers have attempted to reaffirm her agency through their works. As Julee Tate notes in her 2017 article "La Malinche: The Shifting Legacy of a Cultural Icon," works like *Malinche: novela* by Laura Esquivel (2006) emphasize that "the primary focus is not on Malinche's victimhood but rather on the unique position she occupied in the clash of two worlds and the ways in which she used that position to work toward her dream of freedom and self-actualization," (Tate, 2017, p. 85). Yuri Herrera's novella is different from these previous portrayals of La Malinche in that, while it does feature a Malinche-esque figure, it does not feature Malinche herself. By removing the questions of rape and coercion, the question of "her" fellow indigenous people, and the question of national identity, it allows the reader to focus on La Malinche's story as an individual interpreter and to examine the interpreter's visibility and agency when faced with difficult challenges and ethical dilemmas. As Delisle & Woodsworth (1995) point out:

> Indigenous translators consciously or unconsciously become the instruments of foreign domination over their own people, even though they may also try to engage in acts of resistance. Yet power relationships become so unequal that they often have little choice in the matter. (148)

Again, by removing the ties to the conquest, this therefore frees the author to explore these questions without the issue of historical accuracy. La Malinche was a woman so completely bound to the story of Spanish colonial and patriarchal domination that she and Cortés have even been subsumed into the same figure in both Bernal Díaz del Castillo's *True History* and subsequent portrayals of the events of the conquest (Karttunen, 1994, p. 6). As Cypess (1991) mentions: "These works that use the Malinche paradigm as a subtext prove the continuing impact of the image in Mexican culture and point to the need for a revision of the paradigm," (p. 13). I suggest that Herrera's work represents an evolution of this paradigm. By removing La Malinche from the historical context in which she is forever locked into the story of others, Yuri Herrera's *Signs* is able to imagine what La Malinche's story could have looked like had she been given the (fictional) chance to freely exercise her agency as an interpreter.

Despite its short length, Herrera's work is quite complex. *Signs* is the story of Makina, a young woman who has many ties with the historical figure of La Malinche, although these ties are never explicitly pointed out in the novella. In fact, *Signs* relies heavily on inference: the reader infers that the novella is a story about how Makina must travel, with the help of some mafiosos, from a small village in Mexico to the United States in search of her brother who had left to reclaim land supposedly owed to the family. The novella, however, never explicitly names Mexico, Mexico City, the United States, the border, drugs, English, Spanish, etc. Instead, Herrera employs a creative mixture of slang from along the US-Mexico border, circumlocution to avoid using the aforementioned words, and his own invented terms to create a setting that is both real and familiar along the U.S.-Mexico border while simultaneously oneiric and timeless. Adding to the mythical element of the novella is the fact that Herrera structured each chapter around the nine stages a soul must pass through on its way to the underworld in Aztec mythology. This element allows for an alternative reading, one in which Makina has already died from the beginning of her journey, and her travels are not that of the migrant interpreter traveling north to find her brother but rather those of a soul on its way to its final resting place. In this sense, the novella could also be considered another "translation" of La Malinche. As Godayol (2012) describes, "Both the experience of a historical figure and the original meaning of a translated text are subject to the filtering of voices, echoes, intertexts. They never reach us from one sole source but through many rewritings" (p. 71). Therefore, *Signs* also becomes the story of the afterlife of La Malinche.

Signs can be considered a work of transfiction because of Makina's work as an interpreter and her overt connections with La Malinche. Makina's name is resonant of what the colonial Spaniards called Malinche (Doña Marina) as well as the word "maquila:" the assembly plants dotting the U.S.-Mexico border that mostly employ women, often in dangerous conditions. This choice of name is possibly a tongue-in-cheek reference to the previously discussed trope of the work of an interpreter as machine-like. Additionally, like the Malinche, Makina is constantly sexualized; she works as an interpreter, mediator, and go-between in her home village at the local switchboard; and speaks three languages (the novella refers to these as "anglo tongue," "latin tongue," and "native tongue," what the reader infers to be English, Spanish, and a native Mexican language, respectively). The novella also explicitly connects Makina to the birth of a new language (Herrera, 2015, p. 32), similar to how Malinche has been described as the cultural mother of Mexicans as the mother of the "first" mestizo, the son she bore with Cortés. With these similarities and the character's exceedingly positive portrayal and trajectory in the novella, Makina can and has been read as a "revindication" of the mythologized Malinche figure. As Giovanna Rivero (2017) describes, Herrera uses the mythical figure of the Malinche to redeem Mexico and restore confidence in itself (p. 510). Through Makina, the mythical figure of Malinche is vindicated as she becomes a savior for her people and ushers in a new utopia. A far cry from being a mere helpless victim of her circumstances or a traitorous interpreter, Makina is constantly balancing various demands and incentives throughout her journey in search of her brother. She actively uses her skills, knowledge, and experience to take action and choose her next move, sometimes seemingly breaking her (and interpreters') code of ethics and interpreting "unfaithfully," but always for the benefit of her community. She performs out of a sense of duty and responsibility towards her community and is portrayed as good almost beyond reasonable belief–a Virgin of Guadalupe figure rather than a Mexican "Eve." In this way, Makina both redeems La Malinche and demonstrates how it is possible to exercise agency as an interpreter and how to be fulfilled in her profession without the need to find her "own" voice. Additionally, interpreting is shown as a central and vital labor in the novella rather than secondary work. Interpreting is not only central to the plot, but essential for maintaining community ties among the migrants as the novella repeatedly insists.

Interpreters, power, and ethics

Malinche's story is dependent on outside forces. It is unlikely that history would have remembered La Malinche if it were not for the arrival of the Spaniards, and as Karttunen points out (1994, pp. 76-78), many noblewomen in Aztec society were raised to be obedient and demure. As such, the names of many of La Malinche's indigenous contemporaries with a similar social status in indigenous Mexican society have been lost to history. Like Malinche's story, the act of interpreting is similarly dependent on others. While today, interpreters are still seen intermingling with the upper echelons of government and facilitating diplomacy between powerful actors, as Deslile and Woodsworth so elegantly describe, "...translators [and interpreters] have power only by delegation, and only for as long as they can be trusted. Theirs is a second-hand authority that remains circumscribed" (pp. 131-132). Due to this "second-hand authority", interpreting is exclusively dependent on those who need it to be performed. There is no interpreting without the original utterance. Additionally, as Lawrence Venuti (2008) famously discussed in *The Translator's Invisibility: A History of Translation*, the expectations for a "good" translation include that the translator's involvement should not be noticeable to the native English reader. Expectations for interpreters also include a similar level of invisibility. For example, when the general public thinks of interpreters, they often picture conference interpreters. These interpreters are usually located behind the proceedings, existing only behind a glass booth and as a soft voice over a headset. While La Malinche is closer to an escort or community type of interpreter whose physical presence in the interpreter-mediated event is much more apparent, interpreter norms still emphasize minimal involvement in the content of the messages being relayed. Shlesinger (2001) points to this conflict between the inevitable visibility versus invisibility paradox in interpreting in her response to Andre Chesterman and Rosemary Arrojo's 2000 article "Shared Ground in Translation Studies" when she explains:

> This term *interpreting*, however, is weighed down by some oppressive epistemological baggage: its distinctly non-essentialist homologue, to interpret, implies, by definition, that meanings are inherently non-stable, that they have to be *interpreted* in each individual instance, and hence that the translator [*interpreter*] is inevitably visible. (p. 166; emphasis in the original)

Interpreter codes of ethics from professional societies similarly emphasize conduct that minimizes the other participants' awareness of the interpreter, requiring faithfulness and fluidity in order to facilitate proceedings. For example, the current *National Code of Ethics for Interpreters in Health Care* from The National Council on Interpreting in Health Care [NCIHC] mandates that "The interpreter strives to render the message accurately, conveying the content and spirit of the original message, taking into consideration its cultural context," as well as that "The interpreter maintains the boundaries of the professional role, refraining from personal involvement," (2004, p. 3). However, just three points later, the same Code professes that "When the patient's health, well-being, or dignity is at risk, the interpreter may be justified in acting as an advocate," (NCIHC, 2004, p. 3). With these ostensibly conflicting directives for interpreters, it becomes obvious that the grey area between "refraining from personal involvement" and "acting as an advocate" is larger and more complex than the public, and certainly, even many practitioners, may think.

Given this increased visibility of the interpreter and the (sometimes) accepted role of the interpreter as an advocate despite the norms that attempt to obscure their involvement, it comes as no surprise that the interpreter's delegated power and involvement become suspect. This is perhaps why it has become somewhat of a trope in transfiction featuring interpreters to include power-hungry, selfish, and suspect translators (much like how La Malinche has been portrayed throughout history). For example, in Klaus Kaindl and Karlheinz Spitzl's 2014 anthology *Transfiction: Research into the Realities of Translation Fiction*, both Spitzl (2014, pp. 103-112) and Ingrid Kurz (2014, pp. 211-212) discuss translators who break a standard interpreter's code of ethics for personal gain.

Based on all these often-times competing demands and responsibilities placed on interpreters, a new way forward that acknowledges the agency and humanity of the interpreter, one that recognizes that the interpreter is inevitably visible and not a machine, is needed. As Jonathan Downie discusses in his 2016 book, to be a successful interpreter, it is better to focus on the "power" that an interpreter has in the situation rather than trying to achieve the impossible complete neutrality set forth in many interpreter codes of ethics. Downie writes: "Rather than attempt to hide ourselves in the background, this view of interpreting puts front and center our role as those who are actively *helping* clients do their work and achieve their goals," (pp. 6-7; emphasis mine). What makes Yuri Herrera's *Signs* unique is the fact that with the portrayal of the Malinche-esque character, it does not seem to portray a self-interested interpreter, but acknowledges these paradoxes of visibility versus invisibility and advocacy versus non-involvement. The novella offers Makina as a character who consistently employs her agency as an interpreter, much in the way that Downie describes as a way to help their clients (in this case, her community). In this way, the novella shows how interpreting can be performed while exercising individual agency, reflecting and recognizing the complex reality of seemingly opposing demands on interpreters. Additionally, as a community interpreter, Makina is also able to realistically serve as an advocate and activist for those for whom she interprets, and her portrayal as an activist interpreter becomes an example that addresses an enormous power imbalance in situations that involve an interpreter.

Makina as an "activist interpreter": Rehabilitating La Malinche

Early in the novella, the narrator acknowledges the norms of invisibility and non-involvement in interpreting by highlighting Makina's own personal code of ethics with a prominent formatting choice of indenting each line. Makina takes a package of what is presumably drugs from a group of mafiosos in exchange for their help in getting across the border. Makina accepts the package without inspecting it, saying of her profession:

You don't lift other people's petticoats.
You don't stop to wonder about other people's business.
You don't decide which messages to deliver and which to let rot.
You are the door, not the one who walks through it. (Herrera, 2015, pp. 6-7)[9]

---

[9] Henceforth, page numbers following quotations from *Signs Preceding the End of the World* refer to Herrera in References.

Like other professional Codes of Ethics, Makina's code similarly emphasizes confidentiality, impartiality, and fidelity in the sense of not altering the original message. With this assertion, it becomes evident that Makina believes it would be against her own ethics to assert her individual "agency," to insert herself into the conversation, to wonder about the "why" behind the messages, or to take an active role in deciding which messages to convey and which ones to leave alone. Yet, while Makina may hold herself to these rules, it doesn't mean that she's completely helpless. As Downie emphasizes, her position requires her to use her skills and experience to make the most prudent decisions (2016, p. 6). Additionally, Makina's sense of responsibility toward her community makes her an interpreter like the ones described by Kurz, who use their skill to help their people rather than for their own personal gain (2014, pp. 207-210; 212-215), in stark contrast to many earlier portrayals of La Malinche or to the interpreter as a traitor to their own group (as with the Todorova example).

In another departure from previous works of transfiction that portray interpreting as a secondary activity, *Signs* emphasizes the central role of a translator in the migrant community. Herrera highlights how Makina's actions as an interpreter lead to the pacification of different parts of the community, as well as how her actions reverse power imbalances both between members within the community and outside of it (p. 7). Despite the code of fidelity and loyalty that interpreters profess to follow, interpreting, or in some cases, non-interpreting, can become a powerful tool to connect with other members of the shared community and to reverse linguistic hierarchies, putting the monolingual speaker at a significant disadvantage, as we see in this novella. While some interpreter characters gain material and social capital for themselves (see Spitzl (2014), Kurz (2014), here Makina works selflessly. Yet, with this selflessness, her importance to the community as a member and ally is emphasized. Right from the beginning of the novella, even before Makina leaves in search of her brother, Makina's role as intermediary in her community is emphasized in the political and social dealings of the Pueblito: "Through her, the top dogs assured surrender here and sweet setups there, no bones about it; thus, everything was resolved with discreet efficiency," (p. 7). Because of her work, bloodshed between two rival gangs is effectively avoided and the local politics are sorted. Makina is aware of how important her role as a translator in the community is, and this sense of responsibility is often the most important factor in her decisions along her journey in search of her brother. She often cites these responsibilities as the reason why she cannot stay on the other side and must return. Here again we see that instead of frustration at being "just a translator/interpreter" as Ben-Ari (2010) has found in several other interpreter-characters including those in Fuentes's "The Two Shores," *The Interpreter*[10] by Néstor Ponce, *The Mission Song* by John le Carré, and *The Interpreter* by Suzanne Glass, Makina is selfless and recognizes the centrality of her role and its importance for maintaining a community across borders. By using her role as interpreter and the linguistic and cultural knowledge that comes with it, she's specifically helping to keep members of the community together.

Often, because of Makina's dedication to her community, her choices to intervene by interpreting in a way that might normally violate interpreter codes of ethics result in a power reversal. For example, after her long bus journey to the border and right before Makina crosses the river to the other side, she encounters many other migrants attempting to do the same. Two of these migrants happen to be the same two young men who she had forcefully stopped from sexually harassing her during the bus ride to the border. Makina also comes across two *coyotes* (smugglers who bring migrants into the United States illegally). Since she understands what they are saying in Anglo tongue and knows that they are planning to use the two young men as bait for the border patrol while the *coyotes* actually help another group to cross who are paying them more, Makina is able to let the two men know that the coyotes are planning to trick them (p. 16). Due to the fact that Makina is not technically working as an interpreter for the two young men or the *coyotes,* Makina overhearing and sharing this information would be in violation of both confidentiality clauses as well as her own code to not "decide which messages to deliver and which to let rot" (p. 6). However, in stark opposition to La Malinche's portrayal as a Mexican "Eve," known for ushering in original sin in the selfish pursuit of her own knowledge and betraying humanity, Makina is again cast as the savior here as she does the right thing for her community despite the fact that these two nameless characters had attempted to assault her not too long before. Thus, in this way, Malinche, as a traitor, is redeemed, and the power that an interpreter holds becomes apparent. By interpreting the words for the two young men, Makina takes power away from the authority figures and gives it to the migrants, thereby allowing them to make fully informed decisions regarding their safety along their journey, similar to how Del Castillo (1974) has argued that the historical La Malinche operated.

In the most dramatic scene of the novella, in which Makina and several migrants are rounded up and harassed by a bigoted police officer, the power of the interpreter is again emphasized. Through Makina's act of service to her community that could once again go against the rules and expectations for

---

[10] *El intérprete.*

translators and interpreters, both the interpreter and the disadvantaged migrants become visible as human beings in the eyes of the officer. Makina achieves the trope of what Ben-Ari (2010, p. 228) described as being so desirable for translator/interpreter-characters: she finds her own voice and writes her own ironic message to an authority figure. Yet unlike other characters included in Ben-Ari's survey, Makina is able to do so without leaving her role of interpreter. In response to the harassment against one worker in particular, whom the officer had found to have been carrying a book of poetry, Makina, without being asked, takes the worker's notebook and writes a message to force the police officer to leave. However, the message itself is ironically construed in very negative terms that end by effectively taking on the disparaging labels attributed to Makina and the group of migrants:

> We are to blame for this destruction, we who don't speak your tongue and don't know how to keep quiet either. [...] We who came to take your jobs, who dream of wiping your shit, who long to work all hours. [...] We the barbarians. (p. 51)

This self-deprecating message read aloud by the officer is ultimately effective because, by reaffirming her own "abjection," Makina is able to discredit the officer and silence him (Joliff, 2017, p. 100). Makina takes the officer's authority by interpreting/translating his own bigoted thoughts and having him hear them in his own voice. Paradoxically, Makina has exercised agency and broken out of her role as interpreter by taking contestational action and writing her own message against the repressive actions of the officer. She has transformed from an interpreter/translator to an author. However, the negative and self-deprecating nature of that message, coupled with Makina's community-oriented actions throughout the novella, make it difficult for the reader to believe they are Makina's true thoughts about the group to which she belongs. It becomes clear these are the thoughts and feelings she assumes of the officer, brazenly thrown in his face and made to be heard aloud to appeal to his humanity. Understood in this way, Makina then remains an interpreter/translator. She is not expressing her own thoughts or using her own voice to speak to them, but interpreting the thoughts of the officer. However, because Makina has partially remained in her role as interpreter yet seemingly broken her ethics again, she is able to exercise her agency as an interpreter to help her community. Through this paradox, Makina, therefore, becomes an interpreter-activist. This portrayal of Makina as an activist interpreter is more akin to what Rosemary Arrojo has described as transfiction as activism in her evaluation of Rodolfo Walsh's 1967 short story "Footnote."[11] In this subcategory of transfiction, the portrayal of the translator/interpreter insists on making this traditionally subjugated and invisible figure visible. Within transfiction as activism, "…the story constitutes a memorable space for the exploration of the hierarchical opposition between the elite and the subaltern" (Arrojo, 2018, p. 44). Similarly, with Makina's confrontation with the police officer, the "hierarchical opposition" of authority figure versus migrant and authority figure versus interpreter becomes starkly apparent. Unlike in "Footnote," however, with the successful outcome of Makina's intervention, *Signs* presents a concrete case of successful "resistance and empowerment for and in the margins" (Arrojo, 2018, p. 44), not just its possibility. Thanks to Makina's "activist" intervention, both she and the other migrants are free to leave unharmed.

To add complexity to this paradox of the interpreter both gaining her own authorial voice and maintaining her "inferior" position of interpreter with the same action, almost immediately following the scene with the officer, the novella abruptly ends with Makina being taken into a warehouse of sorts in which she is given a new identity. It is reasonable to interpret this ending as the violent, ultimate loss of agency: losing one's own individual identity as a singular subject and being made to be someone else. Indeed, the narrator says, "I've been skinned, she whispered" (p. 56). However, the novella again takes the "both, and" approach by presenting this ending not as a decidedly negative one but one of peaceful acceptance with an eye to the needs of the community at large:

> …she stopped feeling the weight of uncertainty and guilt; she thought back to her people as though recalling the contours of a lovely landscape that was now fading away: the Village, the Little Town, the Big Chilango, all those colors, and she saw that what was happening was not a cataclysm; (p. 56)

Pointedly, it is important to note that in this complex presentation of an interpreter's agency, what ultimately provides Makina with a sense of calm throughout this process of losing her individual identity is the thought of "*her* people." After first acknowledging feeling a sense of anxiety at this process of no longer being the same individual Makina always thought herself to be, the novella ends by emphasizing the comfort she feels in her connections to and role within her community. *Signs* is unique in that it presents both realities existing at the same time regarding the interpreter's agency rather than emphasizing a decidedly negative outcome that denies the ability to receive

---

[11] "Nota al pie".

any sort of individual fulfillment through exercising the profession as is the case with "Footnote." After Makina rescues the other migrants with her interpreting, she has fulfilled her duty and ceases to exist as herself. Yet it's not a tragic ending for her because she is so community-minded, and her goals have been fulfilled. In this way, interpreting can be fulfilling. Therefore, through this ending for Makina, Herrera evolves and redeems the paradigm of La Malinche by showing a Malinche-esque character as a savior for her community rather than as a traitor and a character who was given the fulfilling choice to exercise her agency as an interpreter on her own terms.

Conclusion

With Yuri Herrera's short but impactful novella *Signs Preceding the End of the World*, he is able to tackle the questions of how to adequately represent the complexities of interpreter power and agency as well as how to evaluate the legacy of one of history's most debated interpreters. While the historical Malinche has been variously judged as a traitor, a selfish sexual deviant, a feminist symbol, and a cultural mother to the Mexican and Chicanx people, by removing her from the context of the conquest and providing her with a new interpretation of the long line of "texts" mediating how history understands her, Herrera is able to both contest the negative stereotypes applied to La Malinche in particular and interpreters in general, as well as provide an image of what the interpreter as a powerful ally can look like. Herrera also creatively tackles the paradoxical issues of interpreter ethics and the interpreter's visibility versus their invisibility. By reflecting the unresolved debate in interpreting between non-involvement and advocacy, the novella acknowledges that in these particular situations of an extreme power imbalance, advocacy may be the most appropriate and ethical way for the interpreter to exercise their agency. In this way, *Signs* offers an exciting portrayal of an interpreter as well as a creative re-interpretation/re-translation of La Malinche for the modern reader.

References

Arrojo, R. (2018). *Fictional translators: Rethinking translation through literature.* Routledge.

Bâ, A. H. (1999). *L'étrange Destin De Wangrin.* 10 X 18.

Ben-Ari, N. (2010). Representations of translators in popular culture. *Translation and Interpreting Studies, 5*(2), 220–242. https://doi.org/10.1075/tis.5.2.05ben

Chesterman, A., & Arrojo, R. (2000). Shared ground in translation studies. *Target: International Journal of Translation Studies, 12*(1), 151–160. https://doi.org/10.1075/target.12.1.08che

Cypess, S. M. (1991). *La Malinche in Mexican literature from history to myth* (1st ed.). University of Texas Press.

de Sahagún, B., Dibble, C. E., & Anderson, A. J. O. (1950). *General history of the things of New Spain: Florentine codex*. School of American Research; University of Utah. https://catalog.hathitrust.org/Record/001464954

Del Castillo, A. R. (1974). Malintzin Tenepal: A preliminary look into a new perspective. *Encuentro Femenil, 1*(2), 58–78.

Delisle, J., & Woodsworth, J. (Eds.). (1995). *Translators through history*. (1st ed.). John Benjamins Publishing Company.

Díaz del Castillo, B. (1908). *The true history of the conquest of New Spain... From the only exact copy made of the original manuscript... Volume I* (Ac.6172/96). Genaro García. http://www.globalcommodities.amdigital.co.uk/Documents/Details/BL_AC_6172_96_Vol_1

Downie, J. (2016). *Being a successful interpreter: Adding value and delivering excellence*. Routledge.

Esquivel, L. (2006). *Malinche: novela*. Atria Books.

Fuentes, C. (1994). The two shores. In A. J. Mac Adam (Trans.), *The orange tree* (pp. 3–49). Farrar, Straus, and Giroux.

Glass, S. (2001). *The interpreter* (1st U.S. ed.). Steerforth Press.

Godayol, P. (2012). Malintzin/La Malinche/Doña Marina: Re-reading the myth of the treacherous translator. *Journal of Iberian and Latin American Studies, 18*(1), 61–76.

Herrera, Y. (2015). *Signs preceding the end of the world* (L. Dillman, Trans.). & Other Stories.

Jager, R. K. (2015). *Malinche, Pocahontas, and Sacagawea: Indian women as cultural intermediaries and national symbols*. University of Oklahoma Press.

Joliff, T. C. L. (2017). Laberintos fronterizos. In *Waiting for the barbarians* de J.M. Coetzee y *Señales que precederán al fin del mundo* de Yuri Herrera. *Confluencia (Greeley, Colo.), 33*(1), 91–103. https://doi.org/10.1353/cnf.2017.0034

Kaindl, K., & Spitzl, K. (Eds.). (2014). *Transfiction: Research into the realities of translation fiction* (Vol. 110). John Benjamins B.V.

Karttunen, F. E. (1994). *Between worlds: Interpreters, guides, and survivors*. Rutgers University Press.

Kurz, I. (2007). "The fictional interpreter." In *Interpreting studies and beyond. A Tribute to Miriam Shlesinger*, F. Pöchhacker, A. L. Jakobsen & I. M. Mees (eds.), 277–289. Copenhagen Studies in Language. Copenhagen: Samfundslitteratur Press.

Kurz, I. (2014). On the (in)fidelity of (fictional) interpreters. In K. Kaindl & Karlheinz Spitzl (Eds.), *Transfiction: Research into the realities of translation fiction* (Vol. 110, pp. 205–219). John Benjamins B.V.

Le Carré, J. (2006). *The mission song* (1st ed.). Little, Brown and Co.

Paz, O. (1961). *The labyrinth of solitude: Life and thought in Mexico* (L. Kemp, Trans.). Grove Press.

Ponce, N. (1998). *El intérprete* (1. ed.). Beatriz Viterbo Editora.

Rivero, G. (2017). *Señales que precederán al fin del mundo* de Yuri Herrera: Una propuesta para un *novum* ontológico latinoamericano. *Revista*

Iberoamericana, 83(259), 501–516. https://doi.org/10.5195/REVIBEROAME R.2017.7515

Shlesinger, M. (2001). Shared ground in interpreting studies too. *Target: International Journal of Translation Studies, 13*(1), 165–168. https://doi.org/ 10.1075/target.13.1.14shl

Spitzl, K. (2014). Taking care of the stars: Interpreted interaction in Amadou Hampâté Bâ's *L'étrange destin de Wagrin.* In K. Kaindl & K. Spitzl (Eds.), *Transfiction: Research into the realities of translation fiction* (Vol. 110, pp. 103–112). John Benjamins B.V.

Tate, G., & Turner, G. H. (2002). The code and the culture: Sign language interpreting—In search of the new breed's ethics. In F. Pöchhacker & M. Shlesinger (Eds.), *The interpreting studies reader* (pp. 373–383). Routledge.

Tate, J. (2017). La Malinche: The shifting legacy of a transcultural icon. *The Latin Americanist 61*(1), 81-92. https://www.muse.jhu.edu/article/703570.

The National Council on Interpreting in Health Care. (2004). *A national code of ethics for interpreters in health care.* https://www.ncihc.org/assets/z2021 Images/NCIHC%20National%20Code%20of%20Ethics.pdf

Todorova, M. (2014). Interpreting conflict: Memories of an interpreter. In K. Kaindl & K. Spitzl (Eds.), *Transfiction: Research into the realities of translation fiction* (Vol. 110, pp. 221–231). John Benjamins B.V.

Valdeón, R. (2013). Doña Marina/La Malinche: A historiographical approach to the interpreter/traitor. *Target: International Journal of Translation Studies, 25.* https://doi.org/10.1075/target.25.2.02val

Venuti, L. (2008). *The translator's invisibility: A history of translation* (2nd ed.). Routledge.

Walsh, R. (1981). Nota al pie. In *Rodolfo Walsh: Obra literaria completa* (pp. 419-446). Siglo XXI Editores S. A.

Chapter 3

Intervention as a Form of Survival: Suki Kim's *The Interpreter*

Irem Ayan

The University of British Columbia

Abstract: In *The Interpreter*, a 2003 novel by Suki Kim, a young female court interpreter based in New York City is haunted by the memory of her parents' shocking death. Kim portrays Suzy Park, the interpreter, as someone in a state of emotional distress and racial melancholy. Amidst debilitating tensions of interpreting between lies and secrets, Suzy needs to function as an invisible actor. As the events unfold, she chooses to become highly visible, subverting the norms of neutrality. In some contexts, she takes sides with Korean witnesses. In others, she decides to covertly manipulate the communication, pretending that she is just translating the attorney's questions. This chapter examines Suzy's intentional violation of the main tenets of interpreting practice as stimulating material for reflection on how codes of ethics can be subverted beneath the surface of an impartial and invisible interpreter. Suzy's transgressive acts can be read as a sociological insight by which one can shed light on not only the untenable nature of professional codes of ethics but also on what interpreters can do between, and sometimes even during, utterances to defend their own interests, professional image, reputation, and mental health in racially and gender-biased situations.

Keywords: court interpreting, ethnographic fiction, gender, subversion, Kim

***

Introduction

The use of translators and interpreters as protagonists in fiction has a long tradition (see Kaindl & Spitzl, 2014). Although their representations as fictional beings reflect an immense diversity, interpreters are usually portrayed as characters struggling with existential questions both in their private and professional lives, as exemplified for instance by Nadja, the protagonist in Ingeborg Bachmann's short story *Simultan* (2002). Interpreters' identity crisis and feelings of alienation closely linked to their professional status are characterized as a precondition to being able to function as an interpreter (see Schopohl, 2008). Interpreters are tasked with rendering other people's ideas and words by putting their own thoughts aside. Furthermore, female interpreters are at times illustrated as women in "frivolous relationships" (Simon, 1996a, p. 58, my translation) having sexual affairs with colleagues or either married and/or separated but not yet divorced men, as portrayed in Katie Kitamura's fairly recent novel *Intimacies* (2021). In addition to these characteristics, they also sometimes appear as nameless protagonists, as is the case in Christine Brooke-Rose's *Between* (1968); they are completely "immersed in alien discourse" (p. 421) as they search for a sense of belonging which can be read as a strong reference to the interpreter's invisibility.

Drawing on Michael Cronin's *Translation Goes to the Movies* (2009), which uses the genre of film to discuss questions of culture, identity, conflict, and representation in translation, Kurz (2014) argues that works of film and fiction represent a valuable source because "they reflect—and to a certain extent shape and reinforce—perceptions of our profession" (p. 205). Although the fictional representations of interpreters resonate for the most part with the language of norms of ethics and professional guidelines, there are a few valuable and exceptional examples of manipulation on the part of the interpreter which provide a real-life glimpse into the reality of interpreting practice (see Kurz, 2014).[1] The fictional interpreters' infidelity can be read as a sociological insight that contradicts the unrealistic oversimplification of the interpreter's task as introduced and imposed by the codes of ethics. Against this backdrop, in this chapter, I will first look at how Suzy's initial description as an invisible interpreter adhering to the codes of ethics contradicts her behaviors later in the novel. I will then analyze her marginalized position as a gendered and racialized immigrant interpreter in contemporary white America. Suzy's marginalized position provides her with a unique agency, highlighting the interpreters' position as social participants who can make a difference in an interpreted encounter. Suzy's sense of individual agency emerging from her marginalized status provides her with the tools to carefully perform acts of resistance and transgression under the cloak of invisibility. It also prevents her infidelity from being noticed in the eyes of her clients. Suki

---

[1] Kurz (2014) analyzes the examples of infidelity either due to the interpreter's lack of skills or willingness to fool the users of interpreting services in *The Adventures of Sherlock Holmes* (Cox, 1985), *A Heart so White* by Javier Marías (1995), *Astérix et les Goths* (Goscinny & Uderzo, 1963), the Italian film *Life is Beautiful* (Benigni, 1997), and Sofia Coppola's movie *Lost in Translation* (2003). Suki Kim's *The Interpreter* (2003a) also briefly appears in Kurz's (2014) analysis.

Kim's depiction of Suzy's role and behaviors is inspired by her own short-term personal experience with interpreting in various depositions. In that sense, Kim's novel represents a form of "ethnographic fiction" (Schmidt, 1984) and differs to a great extent from traditional representations of translators and interpreters, allowing us to examine court interpreting through the lens of gendered and racialized labor, which can be subverted and maneuvered via various acts of intervention and transgression.

Fictional neutrality

Early in the novel, we are readily reminded that the protagonist abides by the main tenets of translation and interpreting practice such as "invisibility" (Venuti, 2008), "neutrality," "impartiality," and "accuracy" (see NAJIT Code of Ethics and Professional Responsibilities), as well as "loyalty," "integrity," and "fidelity" of interpretation (see AIIC Code of Professional Ethics).[2] Suzy's adherence to these key concepts is reinforced through two metaphors. First, Kim draws a link between Suzy's job and that of a computer, implying the neutral machine metaphor. Suzy's professional role makes her "feel like the buxom communication officer in *Star Trek*, the one who repeats exactly what the computer says" (p. 14).[3] Suzy needs to approach language as if it were a math question because "an interpreter is like a mathematician" (p. 91) who instantly needs to match every uttered word with its equivalence in the target language. Suzy renders others' utterances and ideas verbatim, displaying no emotional engagement with the people for whom she interprets. She can transmit the meaning without internalizing its context and emotions. In the same vein, being completely aware of the principle of non-involvement and anonymity required by her position, Suzy is more than fine with functioning like a "shadow" (p. 12). As a matter of fact, for her to be invisible is "simpler, freer to be exact" (p. 14). Belonging to neither side in an interpreted context brings her a curious relief. She receives a call when her interpreting services are needed, and the agency sends her the freelancer's contract. All she needs to do is show up at the designated location of the deposition to which she is assigned. In accordance with the contract, which overtly tells her "never to

---

[2] Codes of Ethics and Professional Responsibilities spelled out by the US-based National Association of Judiciary Interpreters and Translators' (NAJIT) and the most up-to-date professional codes of ethics of AIIC (Association International des Interprètes de Conférence) can be found in the following links: https://najit.org/wp-content/uploads/2016/09/NAJITCodeofEthicsFINAL.pdf [consulted on 22 July 2023] and https://aiic.org/document/10277/CODE_2022_E&F_final.pdf [consulted on 22 July 2023]

[3] Numbers in parenthesis following a quote come from Suki Kim's *The Interpreter* (2003a) unless otherwise specified.

engage in small talk with witnesses" (p.14), the professional motto that Suzy adopted for herself is "shut up and get the work done" (p. 15).

Although Kim's description of Suzy resonates with the essentialist approach to language and its belief in the possibility of translators as neutral subjects producing "reproducible meanings that are expected to stay the same, regardless of contexts or circumstances" (Arrojo, 2017, p. 48), there is more than meets the eye in Suzy's seemingly invisible role. Later in the novel, Suzy's position highlights the tension and hardships that underlie interpreting between two languages and cultures. Kim portrays Suzy as someone in a state of emotional distress and racial melancholy, haunted by her parent's mysterious death. Her sense of identity is shattered on both personal and professional levels. Her bilingualism caused persistent feelings of emptiness. Due to her missing sense of belonging, she is floating in a disorienting cultural vacuum. She is torn between her Korean heritage and American upbringing. Her Ivy League college experience contradicts her relatively poor background with her immigrant parents. Within this in-betweenness, Suzy is adept at creatively bridging the cultural and linguistic gaps while being completely disinterested in and detached from the context of her work. Suzy's detachment echoes the need to overcome cultural and linguistic barriers by having to conform to the ethics of professional conduct in practical terms, which "can leave many practitioners with a sense of unease or disorientation" (Baker & Maier, 2011, p. 7). Interpreting within larger social structures, cultural norms, expectations, and ascribed identities can sometimes involve some degree of manipulation in the interpreter's rendering, which leads to a discrepancy between what occurs in the act of interpreting in a given social setting and the standards of practice imposing neutrality and invisibility upon interpreters (see Ayan, 2020). Kim's various plot twists reveal this discrepancy. Framing the act of court interpreting as a performance that is situated in time, space, and a particular social and cultural context, Kim deconstructs the traditional role of the interpreter through a juxtaposition of Suzy's personal interests and her position as a racially underprivileged and gender-subordinated interpreter. If Suzy's Korean background invalidates her membership in the hegemonic American culture, her unique professional position as an interpreter working for the New York City justice system gives her enough tools to not only broach an investigation that had been previously ignored but also go beyond the boundaries drawn by the hierarchies of gender and race.

Gendered and racialized interpreter

The link between the pre-existing socio-cultural expectations and how Suzy is perceived as a professional interpreter by those who use her interpreting services provides a useful lens through which to understand her racialized and gendered status at work. It is crucial to look at Suzy's marginalized position first—both in her private and professional life—in order to examine her reactions to the norms and ethics of interpreting. Drawing a link to Hoagland's *Lesbian Ethics* (1988), which presupposes not privileged agency but rather agency under oppression, I argue that the embeddedness of power relations in Suzy's role creates a certain sense of unique agency for her as well as a shift in her consciousness with regards to maneuvering her disadvantaged position within the context of interpreting practice.

As far as her private life is concerned, Suzy is an attractive woman in her late twenties, living a luxurious life in New York City. However, she does not have a steady income. Thanks to her rich and older boyfriends, she is usually overdressed and wears clothes "sleek enough for any Hollywood starlet" (pp. 3–4) that cost twice her rent. Despite her modishness, her female-coded vulnerability as being "Cinderella-at-midnight" (p. 4) is made clear in the beginning. Additionally, we learn that before working as an interpreter, Suzy had some experience in waitressing, which required too much smiling. She tried faking a smile a couple of times, but it did not work. Eventually, she got fired for her inadequate smiling as well as for "refusing to pretend to be Japanese" (p. 12). She not only refused to perform the gendered image of a nice, friendly, and compassionate service worker, or "emotional labor" in Hochschild's (2003) terms, but also denied to surrender to stereotypes in the American context.[4]

Suzy cannot escape her gendered and racialized status in the context of interpreting either. Kim places her examination of white racism and sexism in contemporary America at both personal and intuitional levels through Suzy's explicitly gendered, embodied, and racialized experience at work. Positioned between the two hierarchized worlds of white America and Korea Town in New York City, Suzy is hired by the New York justice system to interpret for immigrants of Korean origin. She feels the weight of assisting the American justice system where hegemony and the norms of professional practice

---

[4] Through her ethnographic exploration of the experience of modern-day flight attendants and bill collectors, Hochschild (2003) defines emotional labor as "the management of feeling to create a publicly observable facial and bodily display" (p. 7). In other words, emotional labor is the process of policing feelings, facial and bodily expressions to fulfill the specific emotional requirements of a job. Emotional laborers mask, hide, or suppress emotions they feel, or display emotions they do not feel in order to create a suitable professional countenance and behavior.

converge.[5] In her own words, "the interpreter, as much as her heart might commiserate with her fellow native speaker, is always working for the other side" (p. 15). When she arrives at the Bronx criminal court for an interpreting assignment, she becomes—one more time—painfully aware of the stark reality of the racial hierarchy embedded in her work:

> Everyone around her seems to be black, including the security guards, the guys in handcuffs being led by officers, and the rest in line, whose purpose for being here God only knows. Attorneys, though, often are not black. Judges, almost never. None of them are here. They must use a separate entrance, hidden in the back. The power structure is pretty clear. Between those who get locked up and those who do the locking is a colored matter. There are no two ways about it. (p. 87)

Within such a hierarchy, Suzy sometimes finds herself succumbing to lawyers' requests and having to deal with their gendered remarks of a disturbing nature while trying to abide by the norms of interpreting practice. Highlighting the link between Korean last names and their link to class status, Kim (2003b) notes that many Americans think that all Koreans are named Kim, given that Koreans put their last names first and often skip their first names altogether. Confused by this cultural specificity during interrogations, American lawyers tell Suzy to "do it in the American way" (p. 92) and ask her to put first names first, an American demand with which Suzy deals each time. In another example, one of the American lawyers at the court facetiously draws an analogy between her name and Suzie Wong, the beautiful Chinese sex worker in *The World of Suzie Wong* (Quine, 1960), indicating an imagined and constructed figure of female interpreters as sexually available objects, albeit within the terms of hegemonic monogamous heteronormativity.

At times, Suzy must confront attorneys who do not address her directly and even treat her as their personal assistant or secretary. She states that "oddly enough, Korean lawyers are the worst" (p. 265), thinking that it might be linked to Korea's long history of class hierarchy, which reflects the gendered position that women possess in patriarchal societies. In another assignment, a Korean attorney tells Suzy to bring him a cup of coffee during a break, associating her professional role with traditionally female-gendered characteristics. Instead of tending to his sexist request, Suzy refuses to perform

---

[5] Drawing on Gramsci's (1999) notion of "hegemony," some scholars in the field of interpreting studies have highlighted how interpreters—via their interpretations—were actively involved in propagating the ideology and hegemonic force of the institutions for which they are working (see Beaton, 2007, and Zwischenberger, 2016).

the traditional role of a subservient interpreter and just leaves. Labeling this incident as "bullying," Suzy thinks that it is used for a reason:

> Sometimes bullying is a legal tactic to prevent a witness from being questioned: to get the interpreter mad and bust the deposition. A cheap trick, but works. Most depositions never get rescheduled. They cost too much. Before the second try, the case gets settled. (p. 265)

It is not difficult to find parallels in real life. In interpreting, often considered a feminized occupation (see Gentile, 2016, and Ryan, 2015), interpreters are indeed frequently expected to perform tasks that are gendered. Suzy's experience above echoes the testimonies of the conference interpreters whom Spânu (2011) and Ayan (2020) interviewed. Spânu (2011) highlights that interpreters working in the Romanian freelance market are referred to as "girls who translate" (p. 181) by their male clients regardless of their age and education level and are asked in a humorous manner whether they are going to offer a "striptease session" (p. 182) given the amount that they charge for their interpreting services. In a similar vein, drawing on Hochschild's (2003) theory of emotional labor which involves taking care of clients' emotions in interactive service work, Ayan (2020) concludes—in her interviews conducted with twenty-one conference interpreters based in various places in Europe, Asia, and North America—that female interpreters often find themselves in contexts in which they are asked by their clients to carry out irrelevant tasks such as "bringing coffee, tea, or fruits for them" (p. 141). In this sense, Kim's portrayal of Suzy's ambivalent role—as perceived and understood by her clients—represents an important reference to the interpreter's ill-defined role and corresponds to the arguments of Inghilleri (2005) who states, underlining Bourdieu (1977), that interpreters function in "zones of uncertainty" (p. 5), and that they are positioned in the gaps or spaces between fields, lacking clear social definition. Such ambiguity makes interpreters socially vulnerable professionals and leads them (especially those who are marginalized on the basis of socio-cultural, political, and various identity factors) to create a space for their professional survival and "self-preservation" in Monacelli's (2009) terms.[6]

Suzy struggles with various instances involving culture, social status, and other delineations of identity in her private life as well. In that sense, her

---

[6] Monacelli (2009) argues that conference interpreters tend to consider survival as being their primary goal during the act of interpreting due to the face-threatening nature of their profession.

intimate and risky relationships with married white men are not coincidental.[7] Her first relationship with Damian, a scholar of Asian Arts and the husband of her thesis director, Professor Tamiko, was meant to be a remedy for Suzy and her rootlessness in life. She leaves home to live with Damian in order to escape the unbearable Korean traditional culture of patriarchy. She realizes that becoming an independent person and pursuing her American dream would not be possible without liberating herself from the oppressive patriarchy of her family. She needs to have a sense of belongingness. It does not feel like she belongs to her Korean roots, and Damian provides a safe harbor. Similarly, for Damian, Suzy's exotic body offers the distraction that he needs to take a break from his relationship with his wife. When, at the end of the novel, Suzy runs into him with his new white wife and their baby at the Metropolitan Museum of Art, she remembers what Professor Tamiko—on whose bed she lost her virginity to Damian—told her once about her husband: "*He could never love an Asian woman*" (p. 288, italics in the original). According to Rhee (2020), this accidental encounter between Suzy and Damian further supports the idea that Suzy "has been nothing more than an exotic object of entertainment for the blasé taste of a white man" (p. 166).

After her breakup with Damian, Suzy's relationship with Michael (another older, rich, and married boyfriend who calls her pretty much every day from various European cities after his business meetings) was also supposed to empty her of anything she remembers. Suzy had actually been hired as a backup interpreter for Michael's firm. It was her first assignment as an interpreter. Suzy's cool and detached composure attracts Michael's attention. During a break between the executive meetings, Michael initiates a conversation and wonders whether Suzy cannot smile while at work (p. 73). He gives her his business card to see whether she may want to reveal her other face. Suzy's immediate answer, "Forget the call, how about tonight?" (p. 74), bewilders him. Suzy's reaction, which is of a transgressive nature, contradicts Kim's initial description of her as an invisible interpreter as well as her traditional gender role as a woman. Suzy's presence as an attractive female interpreter in an interpreted setting heavily dominated by (white) men generates friction, which is intended. Her body constitutes a point of potential resistance, exhibiting stubbornness within the power relations that come into play in both her professional and private life. Her gendered and racialized position opens up space for resistance, transgression, and subversion. Although

---

[7] It is important to highlight here that Suzy's relationships not only represent a rebellion against her own father's disgust towards interracial dating, but also indicate a strong potential for her to go against the traditional norms both in her personal and professional life.

Michael expects the traditional role of a mistress from Suzy, which involves drama and lots of crying, Suzy displays none of them. After their first lovemaking, Michael turns to Suzy and says that she "was like fucking a ghost, a very sexy one, but a ghost nonetheless" (p. 74). While Suzy's sexual adventures evoke some of the historical suspicions associated with female interpreters, such as promiscuous traitors as in the case of La Malinche, they intersect with and are intensified by her subversive acts violating the norms of interpreting ethics and professional practice as will be explained in detail below.[8]

Survivalist subversion

Kim created her protagonist with a unique position. In contrast to the interpreter's traditionally gendered and marginalized labor relegated to a secondary, subservient, and derivative role (from which Suzy cannot escape), Kim portrays this interpreter as an intelligent woman performing various transgressive acts. As the events unfold later in the novel, Suzy even violates the norms that regulate interpreting practice.

During the course of depositions, there is a constant monologue in Suzy's head, analyzing and commenting on the racial nature of the questions that she is supposed to interpret for Korean witnesses. From her own family's experience, she is completely aware that immigrant life is not easy. When a witness is asked a question about his income, for instance, sometimes he gives an answer that reveals self-incriminating evidence. Immigrant life "follows different rules—no taxes, no benefits, sometimes not even Social Security or green cards" (p. 15), and Suzy knows that very well. In situations like this, one clever way in which Suzy becomes a highly visible interpreter is via direct intervention in Korean to guide the witness through his testimony to help him formulate a diplomatic answer. Hiding behind her Korean language (which is not understood by the American lawyers), Suzy can take sides with the witnesses of Korean origin being more flexible than usual, as her performance during the preliminary interrogation of Mr. Lee (owner of a fruit-vegetable store) demonstrates. After interpreting the assistant district attorney's questions verbatim for Mr. Lee, Suzy adds at the end that he should

---

[8] La Malinche was a Native American woman who worked as an interpreter in negotiations leading to the Spanish conquest of the Aztec Empire. She was Hernán Cortés' interpreter, advisor, and concubine. She is often portrayed as a traitor and treacherous whore who betrayed her people. Her linguistic betrayal, which aided the conquest of an empire, is inextricably linked to the sexual betrayal of her intimate relationship with Cortés. See the discussion about her negative depiction in Louise von Flotow's *Translation and Gender* (2016, pp. 74–76) and Sherry Simon's *Gender in Translation* (1996b, pp. 38–40).

not worry (p. 90) and that he can stop the interrogation to request a lawyer if he desires (p. 91).

In a similar vein, when Korean witnesses panic and struggle to put together an answer to convince the attorney that they are not lying, Suzy can successfully adopt an innocent composure and might come up with an appropriate answer. In the context of war-zone interpreting, Stahuljak (2000) argues that working as an interpreter can mean dealing with conflicting agendas, which can create a violent internal conflict for the interpreter due to being "torn between political allegiance to their [interpreters'] country and professional neutrality, in other words between testimony and translation" (p. 43). Although in the beginning, Suzy admits that the non-involvement aspect of her job is what she likes the most, later in practice, she decides to intervene for the sake of helping disadvantaged Koreans. In this sense, her predicaments correspond to the experiences of interpreters working in asylum situations who find themselves in the middle of conflicting agendas (see Inghilleri, 2003). Suzy embodies the uneasiness experienced by legal interpreters who find that their "*habitus* and capital are closer to those of the defendant than of the legal authorities," as Vidal Claramonte (2005) reminds us (p. 266, emphasis in the original).

In another example, while interpreting a deportation sentence for a woman whose story is very much like that of Suzy's own mother, Suzy needs to deal with the emotional dimension brought about by the situation. Jung Soon Choi, the woman in question, is Suzy's mother's age, used to work as a cashier in a store, and was abused by her husband, similar to the story of Suzy's own family. When Mrs. Choi is asked during the hearing whether it is true that her daughter abandoned her because she could not stand her, Suzy sees the sadness on Mrs. Choi's face and feels as if her own mother is being accused. She pleads to herself silently that the lawyers should leave her alone (p. 269). As Carstensen & Dahlberg (2017) point out, court interpreting is "not only a question of translating emotions (or not) from one language or culture to another but furthermore, the task involves producing in the listener a proper emotional state" (p. 57), which they understand to be a characteristic of emotional labor, echoing Hochschild (2003) and Morris (2010).[9] Suzy decides

---

[9] Drawing our attention to the significant importance attributed to the role of feelings and emotions in the practice of court interpreting, Carstensen & Dahlberg (2017) highlight that the norms of neutrality and objectivity as well as identification with the speaker can create an emotional dimension for the interpreter. They refer to Morris's (2010) "Images of the Court Interpreter" in which she underlines the importance of the court interpreter to adopt the interpreted participants' roles and perspectives, stating that "the interpreter must identify with and *become* each speaker" (p. 31, emphasis mine).

to leave out some of the statements that she is supposed to interpret in order not to extinguish Mrs. Choi's last hope. When Mrs. Choi says that she stabbed a black teenage girl who attempted to rob her store, Suzy hesitates for a few seconds before translating and thinks of softening her statement in English, but in vain. Similar to what she does during Mr. Lee's deposition, she steps out of the boundaries of her neutrality by speaking directly to Mrs. Choi during the court hearing in order to guide her to answer the questions properly because she thinks that there is not much hope for her case. Irritated by this lack of hope and Mrs. Choi's bluntly short sentences, Suzy decides to be even more visible, and intervenes in Korean at the end of attorney's questions by turning to Mrs. Choi, and encourages her to say more, overtly telling her that it might be her last opportunity to say something (p. 271). However, Suzy has to accept the harsh reality and translate the deportation date to the woman, reminding herself that anything can happen because permanent residency does not guarantee permanency (p. 274).

There are a couple of examples of court interpreters who, just like Suzy, decide to spread calm and interpret in favor of their clients. Carstensen and Dahlberg (2017) conclude in a pilot study based on semi-structured interviews with twenty-nine respondents (seventeen interpreters, eight judges, and four legal counselors), from three district courts in Sweden in 2015 and 2016, that "interpreters have a calming effect on their clients," and that "a good interpreter knows how to spread calm in the courtroom," "because the situation in the courtroom can be very tense" (p. 58). Parallels in the context of medical and conference interpreting can also be found. A medical interpreter whom Angelelli (2004) interviewed, for instance, recalls a situation "where she crossed a boundary on the basis of her being a mother" while interpreting for a young man whose "arm had been mangled in a cement mixer" (p. 110). Referring to the young man as "a baby" and reminding herself that she has a daughter herself who is older than him, the interpreter admits comforting the young patient to the best of her ability as a mother, "rubbing his eyebrow the whole time" (Angelelli, 2004, p. 110). In a similar vein, Ayan (2020) argues in the context of conference interpreting that interpreters may indeed choose to step out of the boundaries of neutrality in an attempt to take care of their clients and/or speakers' feelings by performing a form of emotional labor, developing and operationalizing empathy with them. A staff interpreter employed at a government institution whom Ayan (2020) interviewed reveals that in a consecutive interpreting setting, he switched to reported speech mode, thinking that the head of the delegation for whom he was working might not appreciate the original statement. The interpreter did not want his own delegation to think that the statement in question was actually coming from him. In this particular context, the reported speech mode provides the interpreter with a unique tool to distance himself from the content and carefully adjust his rendering "for the sake of his employer's appreciation" (Ayan, 2020, p. 137).

In one instance in the novel, there is a cultural misunderstanding about the Korean way of downplaying the significance of pain. Suzy makes a slight involuntary grimace after hearing the questions from an attorney who puts pressure on a suffering witness, insisting that the latter is lying about his pain because he refused an ambulance and claimed that he was fine at the time of the accident (p. 15). In situations like this, Suzy tries hard not to show her anger (pp. 15–16) and chooses to "embellish truth according to how she sees fit" (p. 16). Although she is aware that she will be fired if anyone notices her bias in her rendering, she decides to subvert the norms of neutrality because she believes that truth can come in different shades. In Suzy's own words, "lawyers with a propensity for Suzy Wong movies may not always see that" (p.16). This statement highlights how Suzy's marginalized and gendered status at work plays an important role in her decision to go against the norms of interpreting practice.

Suzy's most skilled manipulation occurs during the interrogation of Mr. Lee (the fruit and vegetable store owner). Suzy accidentally learns that Mr. Lee was employed at a store a few years ago until the owners were dead. Suzy's parents were killed four years after she was mercilessly disowned by her father because of the shame she caused for her family by choosing to run away with a white man. She steps out of the boundaries of her neutrality by intervening in order to address to Mr. Lee the questions that she made up in Korean, while pretending that she is simply interpreting the attorney's questions. It turns out that Mr. Lee had worked for Suzy's killed parents. Assuming an active role and behaving like a detective, Suzy initiates her own investigation to solve the murder mystery of her parents, which becomes a moral imperative for her to alleviate her traumatized feelings, remove her guilt, and move on with her life. She finds out, thanks to her intervening questions, that it was not a random shooting (as the American detectives who really did not want to deal with the investigation had initially claimed). Within these power structures tainted with racism and sexism, Suzy demonstrates a "rugged individualism" (Rhee, 2020, p. 161) which gives her the courage and strength to go after and implement her own truth. The need to prioritize her own interests and follow her own truth leads Suzy to defy the conventional ethics of interpreting for her own benefit.

Conclusion

The term interpreter carries multiple meanings in Kim's novel. Functioning as an interpreter allows Suzy Park to exist between and navigate through the hybridity and in-betweenness of public vs. private, move between family vs.

friends, maneuver between Korean heritage vs. American upbringing, and negotiate the subculture of the Korean gangs filled with crimes vs. the need to remain professionally transparent and detached. Suzy's investigation of her own parents' killing reinforces the idea that interpreters do not function as neutral and invisible conveyors of meaning between languages as dictated by the professional guidelines of practice, but rather like detectives to understand themselves as well as those for whom they interpret. In this sense, Suzy's professional role as a court interpreter becomes intrinsic to her role as a "metaphysical detective" (Kim, 2009) to make sense of the clues available to solve her parents' mysterious killing. This investigation is also necessary for her to figure out her own existential anxieties. As one of the interpreters whom Angelelli (2004) interviewed states, interpreters indeed dig deep "to get to the hidden and valuable information" (p. 125) in their interpreted contexts.

It is worth highlighting that Suzy acts like a detective to solve a crime in which she is also personally implicated. She finds out from her investigation that her parents were involved in many moral crimes, and her sister, Grace, functioned as an interpreter for her parents throughout the entire process from which Suzy was completely excluded. Suzy's parents acted as informants and reported illegal Korean immigrants to INS (Immigration and Naturalization Service) to secure their children's American citizenship. Suzy later finds out that her parents themselves were also illegal immigrants. Although at the end of the novel Suzy wonders "What the hell's an interpreter if she can't even interpret her own sister?" (p. 293) and thinks that she failed in her task as an interpreter because she could not really interpret her own family members and herself, she eventually proves to be a successful detective-interpreter given her supposedly unethical interventions. She cleverly maneuvered and subverted the norms in order to outwit the white American authorities for her own personal and professional survival.

Kim's portrayal of Suzy as an interpreter-detective overstepping the boundaries of neutrality raises crucial questions and highlights the need to rethink and revisit the main tenets of interpreting practice rather than simply imposing the language of the codes of ethics upon interpreters. Camayd-Freixas (2013) argues that "the moral sentiments of sympathy (empathy), compassion and benevolence are primary to any rationalization of ethics" (p. 24). It is incommensurate to expect interpreters to rationalize ethical behaviors using moral sentiments when they have to suppress emotions to display the neutral performance expected from an interpreter (see also Camayd-Freixas, 2009). The interpreter's professional role implies a constant calibration and adjustment of her rendering and behavior according to the particular social and cultural needs of a given interpreted-mediated event. Suzy's experience therefore provides valuable insights to construct a valid discussion on the reality of interpreters' work. Drawing upon her own experience of working as an interpreter who served in depositions for a limited period of time to research for the novel, Suki Kim herself embodied various speakers while trying to assume a form of neutrality. She experienced translating lies amidst conflicts of interest. In a short news article, she states the following: "The job of being an interpreter helped change my novel's character. I never imagined that it would change me".[10] Kim was once was asked to interpret for a witness who looked familiar to her, she believed a good interpreter would have stopped the questioning right away. However, being a curious fiction writer, Kim accepted the assignment despite the conflict of interest at stake. She highlights that she had no moral quandary about interpreting her witness' lies. Her job was after all to repeat verbatim everything that was said, just as her protagonist Suzy claims in the beginning of the novel. However, Kim also confesses that learning about the other side of the witnesses' story in the context of her work sometimes bothered her to a certain extent, a revelation that she could probably not achieve had she not had a first-hand experience in interpreting in depositions herself.

In line with the above, Kim's ethnographic fiction reveals that although interpreters strive to abide by the norms of invisibility and neutrality while they are in action, they cannot actually escape from becoming involved in the context of their work. Their actions can differ to a great extent from what they think and say about the norms of professional practice. This revelation transforms Kim's reality-inspired novel into a real-world example, making it stand out among traditional representations of female interpreters in fiction. It displays a clear picture of what marginalized interpreters—functioning under a form of oppression tainted by the hegemony of sexist and racist institutions—experience and may encounter at work.

References

AIIC. (2022). Code of Professional Ethics. https://aiic.org/document/10277/CODE_2022_E&F_final.pdf [consulted on 22 July 2023]

Angelelli, C. V. (2004). *Medical interpreting and cross-cultural communication.* Cambridge University Press.

Arrojo, R. (2017). *Fictional translators: Rethinking translation through literature.* Routledge.

Ayan, I. (2020). Re-thinking neutrality through emotional labor: The (in)visible work of conference interpreters. *TTR: traduction, terminologie, rédaction, 33*(2), 125–146.

---

[10] See Kim, S. (2003b). "Translating Poverty and Pain: An Interpreter Glimpses the Hardships Hidden Behind the Walls of Language." *The New York Times.* ProQuest Historical Newspapers. The New York Times with index pg. CY3.

Bachmann, I. (2002). *Simultan: Erzählungen.* Piper.

Baker, M., & Maier, C. (2011). Ethics in interpreter and translator training: Critical Perspectives. *The Interpreter and Translator Trainer, 5*(1), 1-14.

Beaton, M. (2007). Interpreted ideologies in institutional discourse: The case of the European parliament. *The Translator,* 13(2), 271–296.

Benigni, R. (Director). (1997). *Life is beautiful.* Translator of subtitles not credited. (DVD 121 min.), USA: Miramax Films.

Bourdieu, P. (1977). *Outline of a theory of practice.* Cambridge University Press.

Brooke-Rose, C. (1968). *Between.* Michael Joseph.

Camayd-Freixas, E. (2009). Interpreting after the largest ICE raid in U.S. history. In S. Oboler (Ed.), *Behind bars* (pp. 159–173). New York: Palgrave Macmillan.

Camayd-Freixas, E. (2013) Court interpreter ethics and the role of professional organizations. In C. Schäffner, K. Kredens and Y. Fowler (Eds.) *Interpreting in a changing landscape* (pp. 15–30). John Benjamins.

Carstensen, G., & Dahlberg, L. (2017). Court interpreting as emotional work: A pilot study in Swedish law courts. *NoFo,* 14, 45–64.

Claramonte, M. C. Á. V. (2005). Re-presenting the 'real': Pierre Bourdieu and legal translation. *The Translator 11*(2), 259–275.

Coppola, S. (Director) (2003). *Lost in translation.* (DVD 97 min.), USA: Focus Features.

Cox, M. (1985). *The adventures of Sherlock Holmes: The Greek interpreter.* TV series: Season 1, Episode 9. (VHS 50 min.), UK: MPI Media Group.

Cronin, M. (2009). *Translation goes to the movies.* Routledge.

Gentile, P. (2016). Through women's eyes. Conference interpreters' self-perceived status in a gendered perspective. *Hermes – Journal of Language and Communication in Business, 58,* 19–42.

Goscinny, R. & Uderzo, A. (1963). *Astérix et les Goths.* Neuilly-sur-Seine: Dargaud.

Gramsci, A. (1999). *Selection from the prison notebooks.* London: Lawrence and Wishart.

Hoagland, S. L. (1988). *Lesbian ethics: Toward new value.* Institute of Lesbian Studies.

Hochschild, A. R. (2003). *The managed heart: Commercialization of human feeling.* University of California Press.

Inghilleri, M. (2003). Habitus, field and discourse: Interpreting as a socially-situated activity. *Target: International Journal of Translation Studies 15*(2), 243–268.

Inghilleri, M. (2005). Mediating zones of uncertainty: Interpreter agency, the interpreting habitus and political asylum adjudication. *The Translator 11*(1), 69–85.

Kaindl, K., & Spitzl, K. (Eds.) (2014). *Transfiction: Research into the realities of translation fiction.* John Benjamins.

Kim, S. (2003a). *The interpreter.* Picador.

Kim. S. (2003b). Translating poverty and pain: An interpreter glimpses the hardships hidden behind the walls of language. *The New York Times.* ProQuest Historical Newspapers. The New York Times with index pg. CY3.

Kim, S. Y. (2009). Lost in translation: The multicultural interpreter as metaphysical detective in Suki Kim's *The interpreter*. In Pearson, N. & Singer, M. (Eds.) *Detective fiction in a postcolonial and transnational world* (pp. 193–217), Routledge.

Kitamura, K. (2021). *Intimacies*. Riverhead Books.

Kurz, I. (2014). On the (in)Fidelity of (fictional) interpreters. In Kaindl, K., & Spitzl, K. (Eds.) *Transfiction: Research into the realities of translation fiction* (pp. 205–219). John Benjamins.

Marías, J. (1995). *A heart so white* (translated from the Spanish by Margaret Jull Costa). Harvill.

Monacelli, C. (2009). *Self-Preservation in simultaneous interpreting*. John Benjamins Publishing Company.

Morris, R. (2010). Images of the court interpreter: Professional identity, role definitions and self-image. *Translation and Interpreting Studies* 5(1), 20–40.

NAJIT. (2022). Code of ethics and professional responsibilities https://najit.org/wp-content/uploads/2016/09/NAJITCodeofEthicsFINAL.pdf [consulted on 22 July 2023]

Quine, R., Stark, R., Patrick, J., & Mason, R. (Directors). (1960). *The world of Suzie Wong*. (DVD 126 min.), Paramount Pictures.

Rhee, S. K. (2020). Suki Kim's *The interpreter:* A critical rewriting of the hard-boiled detective fiction. *genre, 53*(2), 159-182.

Ryan, R. (2015). Why so few men?: Gender imbalance in conference interpreting. https://aiic.org/document/311/AIICBlog_Jun2019_HICKEY_Women_take_the_mic_in_CI_EN.pdf

Schmidt, N. J. (1984). Ethnographic fiction: Anthropology's hidden literary style. *Anthropology and Humanism Quarterly, 9*, 11-14. https://doi.org/10.1525/ahu.1984.9.4.11

Schopohl, E. (2008). (De-)Constructing translingual identity. Interpreters as literary characters in *simultan* by Ingeborg Bachmann and *between* by Christine Brooke-Rose. *TRANS*. https://doi.org/10.4000/trans.283

Simon, S. (1996a). Entre les langues: *Between* de Christine Brooke-Rose. *TTR: traduction, terminologie, rédaction, 9*(1), 55–70.

Simon, S. (1996b). *Gender in translation*. Routledge.

Spânu, L. (2011). Skirts and suits in conference interpreting: Female interpreters and male clients on the current Romanian market. *Studia UBB Philologia, 1*(6), 175–189.

Stahuljak, Z. (2000). Violent distortions: Bearing witness to the task of wartime translators. *TTR: traduction, terminologie, rédaction, 13*(11), 37–51.

Venuti, L. (2008). *The translator's invisibility: A history of translation*. Routledge.

Von Flotow, L. (2016). *Translation and gender: Translating in the 'era of feminism.'* Routledge.

Zwischenberger, C. (2016). The policy maker in conference interpreting and its hegemonic power. *Translation Spaces, 5*(2), 200–221.

Chapter 4

Unbearable Intimacies: The Implicated Interpreter in Katie Kitamura's *Intimacies*

Yan Wu

University of Massachusetts Amherst

Abstract: Using Katie Kitamura's second transfictional novel *Intimacies* as a case in point, this chapter investigates the life trajectory of the unnamed, transnational, and multilingual interpreter in an intimate space. The narration of the protagonist's experience alternates between her professional role as an interpreter on a short-term contract with the International Criminal Court in The Hague and her personal life as a sojourner with tenuous social relationships while living in that city. This chapter discusses how Kitamura problematizes the normative expectations for the interpreter's role as the invisible and neutral conduit, mainly through her close depictions of the power dynamics surrounding interpreting activities. The interpreter's task is shown to be not only cognitively loaded but also emotionally taxing and ethically challenging. From the first-person narrative point of view of an observant interpreter, the reader can appreciate how the presence and voice of the interpreter could impact interpreted events. In addition, the novel showcases how the interpreter's personal morality gets implicated in the institutional structure of her workplace. The analysis aims to delineate the fictional interpreter's shifting positions from subservience to autonomy through her self-reflexive negotiations with the manipulative forces that permeate her professional and personal life.

Keywords: ethics, interpreter, intimacy, (in)visibility, Kitamura

***

Introduction

Transfiction has been a generative literary genre in which realities and perceptions about translation and interpreting get extended through "an aestheticized imagination of translatorial action" (Spitzl, 2014, p. 364). As

Klause Kaindl, a leading theorist in this field and co-editor of *Transfiction: Research into the Realities of Translation Fiction*, suggests, transfiction brings the topic of translation and interpreting into "a fictional space with a performative act," (2014, p.10) and, for Kaindl:

> a character who is a translator or interpreter as well as translation process can be employed to examine the big questions and opposing poles of communication, such as understanding and misunderstanding, creation and negotiation of meaning, the self and the other, and encounters between languages and cultures. (2014, p. 10)

The use of fiction in examining the phenomena of translation and interpreting has thus opened a comparative space for testing and challenging pre-existing assumptions about translation and the work of translators and interpreters.

Earlier works that investigate the interface of translation and fiction generally follow a twofold perspective: translation, in its various fictionalized forms, functions as a theme or narrative device to construct cultural experiences in literary works; and fiction, when emplotted with the translation process, offers materials for revisiting and advancing translation theories (Pagano, 2002, p. 81). Translation scholars, some of them literary translators themselves, contributed to these early theoretical discussions offering insights regarding authorship/ originality (Steiner 1998; Arrojo 2017), postmodernity (Thiem 1995; Baer 2005), trans-/multilingualism (Beebee 1994; Delabastita & Grutman 2005; Wilson 2011), and the tropes of the translator's (in)fidelity and (in)visibility (Strümper-Krobb 2003; Wakabayashi 2005; Arrojo 2007; Cronin 2009). More recently, translator figures in fiction have been spotlighted as agential beings: the translator in Yoko Tawada's story "St. George and the Translator" uses fragmented literal translations to introduce foreignness to the original (Kaindl, 2014, pp. 87-101); fictional translators in Julio Cortázar's "Carta a una señorita en París [Letter to a Young Lady in Paris] and Rodolfo Walsh's "Nota al pie [Footnotes] choose self-inflicted deaths to make bold statements on their undeniable visibility (Miletich, 2022, pp. 89-108); and two more fictional translators in Moacyr Scliar's "Notas ao pé da página [Footnotes] and Jorge Luis Borges's "Pierre Menard, Author of the Quixote" show their creative agency by negotiating with the dichotomous directions of "approximation" and "autonomy" (Leal, 2023, p. 51).

Alongside these critical explorations, the study of fictional interpreters departs from the ambivalent role of these professionals as "in-between figures, loathed and admired, privileged and despised" (Cronin, 2002, p. 55) and situates the fictional interpreters' dilemmas and actions within a wide array of socio-political conditions. One of the most representative approaches in this regard is utilizing the fictional portrayal of interpreters to gauge against the ethical principles of interpreting, thus challenging normative expectations (such as the interpreter as a conduit) and prescriptive codes (such as neutrality and impartiality). Moira Inghilleri (2012) uses the interpreter's emotional monologue in Cecilia Parkert's *Witness* to critique the expectation of the interpreter's neutrality and calls for a legitimate space for the interpreter's moral subjectivity to intervene in ethically challenging situations; Ingrid Kurz (2014) discusses how fictional interpreters' violation of the fidelity code or their failure to provide faithful renditions (either intentionally or unintentionally) reinstates the interpreter's power to mediate and even manipulate the outcome of communication; Kayoko Takeda (2019) presents multiple cinematic scenarios in which fictional interpreters break away from the code of impartiality and reevaluates the interpreter's agency in the context of personal exposure to violence and moral dilemma.

Katie Kitamura's transfictional work serves as a great example to analyze the ongoing ethical discussions. This chapter first examines the translator's dilemma as a recurring theme in the author's fictionalization of translation and interpreting. The chapter concentrates on Kitamura's most recent novel, *Intimacies*. The novel is narrated by an unnamed, transnational, and multilingual protagonist who is a conference interpreter working at an international war crime tribunal in The Hague. Kitamura problematizes the normative expectation for the interpreter's role as the invisible and neutral conduit through her close depictions of interpreting activities not only as cognitively loaded tasks but also as emotionally taxing and ethically challenging jobs. From the first-person narrative point of view of an observant interpreter, the reader can appreciate how the presence and voice of the interpreter could impact interpreter-mediated events. In addition, the novel showcases how the interpreter's personal morality gets implicated in the institutional structure of her workplace. The analysis aims to delineate the fictional interpreter's shifting positions from subservience to autonomy through her self-reflexive negotiations with the manipulative forces that permeate her professional and personal life.

The translator's dilemma

Katie Kitamura's most recent works of fiction, *A Separation* (2017) and *Intimacies* (2021), both feature language professionals as protagonists; an unnamed literary translator in the former and a conference interpreter in the latter. Kitamura's characters, in the works mentioned, are part of the universal issues related to Translation Studies: (in)fidelity, (in)visibility, subservience, agency, and power struggles. Through alternating accounts of personal and professional spheres, Kitamura showcases how the translator's ethical dilemma may have a spillover effect on one's management of personal and familial issues.

The protagonist in *A Separation* is constantly dealing with the absent presence of her husband as a spectral figure in her life. From the perspective of a first-person narrator, the story depicts the protagonist's trip to Greece, a country that is foreign to her, in search of her separated husband while translating a sample chapter in a novel about a couple whose child disappeared. She plans to ask for a divorce but keeps it a secret from her husband's family. Her trip to Greece, nonetheless, is not out of her own will but arranged by her mother-in-law. The protagonist's husband, who is a writer working on a new book about mourning rituals, is later found to have died unexpectedly from a violent attack. After being informed of the husband's death, the protagonist goes back to the man's hotel room to collect his belongings, including his unfinished book manuscript, which her mother-in-law requests her to gather for potential publication. The formation of this intricate translator-author-patron relationship blurs the boundary between professional and familial roles, thus generating complicated ethical responsibilities. The translator in Kitamura's story, a wife/widow and a daughter-in-law, follows the directives of her mother-in-law and fulfills her moral duties for the family. The process of separation between her, her husband, and his family is incomplete: the marriage and the pending divorce, given the death of the husband, becomes an imminent legal contract bound by loyalty without a real conclusion.

The moral question of fidelity, or as the narrator describes it in plural form, "a question of infidelities" (Kitamura, 2017, p. 2), sits at the center of the tension in the novel. A mixed sense of duty and detachment prevails in the drifting thoughts of the narrator as she talks about her husband's betrayal and suspected affairs, reveals her own romantic relationship with another man, and relates issues in her personal life to the literary translator's task.

> Translators are always worried about being *faithful to the original*, an impossible task because there are multiple and often contradictory ways of being faithful, there is literal fidelity and there is *in the spirit of*, a phrase without concrete meaning. (Kitamura, 2017, p. 186, emphasis in original)

The distinction the narrator makes between literal faithfulness and spiritual faithfulness serves as a self-justification for her own life decisions, manifesting a mood of passivity and undecidedness. The fictional translator keeps the promise to her late husband that their separation would remain a secret. She inherits his money but leaves it untouched. She later gets engaged to another man but remains ambivalent about the commitment to remarry.

The ethical principle of fidelity in *A Separation* functions as a critical nexus for Kitamura to connect personal life and the work of translation analogically, a narrative strategy she continues to utilize in *Intimacies*. The indeterminate zones of human morality are explored once more in a similar setting. In this case, an unnamed female protagonist, an interpreter, is involved in an ongoing marriage/divorce. The novel starts amidst a similar air of disorientation: the reader follows the homodiegetic narrator as she navigates her way into the city of The Hague. The narrator's spatial consciousness signals an ambivalent feeling of familiarity and uncertainty. She leaves New York to work as an interpreter for the International Criminal Court after her father's death and her mother's relocation to Singapore; she is uncertain whether the job or her romantic relationship will sustain her stay in The Hague permanently. She has rented her own apartment and later moves into her boyfriend's apartment, but temporarily lives there alone (the boyfriend is still married and out of the country, presumably on a trip to deal with his divorce). Although she works with five languages professionally, she barely understands the Dutch language she hears on the street. The sojourning status of the protagonist in the city of The Hague makes her presence transitory. Deprived of solid social relationships, the protagonist carries with her a strong sense of rootlessness, in line with what Esperança Bielsa describes as "a ubiquitous condition of homelessness" for a cosmopolitan stranger (2016, p. 47). In contrast to her friends and colleagues, who are all named and seem to be living a more settled life, the nameless protagonist is positioned as a flexible citizen who can move across borders but has lost her footing in any local communities, a partial insider and partial outsider.

The interpreter-protagonist's solitary occupancy of her boyfriend's place showcases the character's negotiation with her (in)visibility. This part of Kitamura's story is reminiscent of the protagonist in Julio Cortázar's short story "Letter to a Young Lady in Paris," in which the translator-narrator reveals how his temporary residence at the young lady's apartment has left unavoidable traces even though he prefers to keep everything as it was. Cortázar's story has been read as "a metaphor of translation," with the translator figure trying to stay invisible but failing to do so (Guzmán, 2006, p. 80). In contrast, Kitamura's interpreter-narrator moves into her boyfriend's apartment at his request and waits for his return as her response to the symbolic affirmation of her significance in his life. Yet, since the man fails to come back within the promised time frame and becomes non-responsive in their daily communication, the protagonist starts to ponder the paradox of her presence. For the narrator, her stay in the apartment is less impactful than the material presence of a photograph of the man's wife on the bookshelf. She gets annoyed by the fact that she has lived in the apartment for a month but changed almost nothing in it; she is present but remains invisible (Kitamura, 2021, p.141).[1] Through the female protagonist's inner struggles for visibility and recognition, Kitamura evokes the interpreter/mistress trope and, more broadly, the traditionally gendered connotations surrounding translation and interpreting as secondary and subservient labor.[2]

Besides using the translator's ethical dilemma as a metaphor for one's personal life, Kitamura dedicates a substantial part of the novel's plot to representing the interpreter's working conditions. Kitamura sets her fictional interpreter-protagonist as a cosmopolitan woman who masters multiple languages: native fluency in English and Japanese (languages spoken in her family), French acquired from her childhood education, and Spanish and German at the level of professional proficiency (p. 13). Even though she is a highly competent and well-qualified language professional, the narrator never regards interpreting as an easy task. From her perspective as a new employee at the International Criminal Court, she observes her colleagues and other professionals at her workplace and tries to internalize the norms of interpreting in the legal and justice setting:

> Interpretation was a matter of great subtlety, a word with many contexts... A trial was a complex calculus of performance in which we were all involved, and from which none of us could be entirely exempt. It was the job of the interpreters not simply to state or perform but to repeat the unspeakable. (p. 16)

The interpreter-narrator highlights the performative nature of the language of the Court and how the interpreter's self can potentially be torn by this task to interpret: a private self that is subject to the emotional burden of dealing with "the intimate nature of pain" and a public self that is an instrumental part of the "complex calculus of performance" within the international justice system (p. 16). For Kitamura and her fictional interpreter, it is precisely in this schism of proximity and distance that the job of interpreting gives rise to multiple layers of overwhelming intimacy.

---

[1] Henceforth, page numbers following quotations from *Intimacies* refer to Kitamura (2021) in References.

[2] The most representative interpreter/mistress figure in history and in literature is La Malinche, the interpreter/concubine of Hernán Cortés during the conquest of Mexico. See Valdeón (2013) for a comprehensive historiographical study of this figure.

Interpreting as an intimate encounter

The notion of intimacy is evoked by Gayatri Chakravorty Spivak (2002) to name translation as "the most intimate act of reading" (p. 370). Spivak describes the literary translator's act as "surrendering" to the text; for her, that kind of reading and surrendering can generate new meanings "in the closest places of the self" (2002, p. 370). Spivak's practice of intimate translation marks her voluntary decision to forego her personal self to get closer to the text and to be fully occupied by the task. Such an intimate space of connection also exists in the practice of interpreting, where the interpreter surrenders her personal "I" to an "alien I"—using the first-person pronoun when interpreting someone else's words.[3] The interpreter's adoption of the "alien I," when viewed as a professional norm, suggests a way of distancing the interpreter's self (including personal values, attitudes, and emotions) away from the "discursive performance of a professional role" (Koskinen, 2020, p. 103). Meanwhile, whether being distanced or alienated enough or not, the first person "I" would make "the boundary between the interpreter and the interpretee porous" (Koskinen, 2020, p. 103). In this sense, the interpreter's use of the "alien I" places the interpreter's self in what Erbu Diriker describes as "a vaguely defined and highly unpredictable communion with the speaker in the same utterance" (2004, p. 138), which inevitably adds to the intimate nature of interpreting practice.

In Kitamura's depiction of an interpreted witness testimony, the interpreter's "I" and the "alien I" are mixed as if they are one narrating voice. The narrator's point of view shifts between the interpreter's personal "I" and the interpreted "I" of the witness— "I paused. Because I wanted to protect my family... No. I paused. When I arrived, my brothers were dead" (p. 184). The indistinguishable first-persons due to the omission of quotation marks leads to an intended effect of confusion on the reader. In this extreme case of retelling a traumatizing story, Kitamura symptomatically demonstrates through her literary language the intimacy of sharing a personal pronoun. The co-existence of the interpreter's personal "I" and the adopted "alien I" showcases that they cannot be neatly separated. The interpreter-narrator in the novel continues to reflect on the interference caused by this subtle interaction:

---

[3] Anthony Pym (2012) mentions the translators' use of the "alien I" as a symbolic sacrifice for "the interests of illusory communication with a so-called source text" (p. 45). The "alien I" as a pronominal form has also been associated with discussions about the translator's authorship. See Pym (2011) and Jansen (2019).

As I looked down at the witness, it prickled through me, the strangeness
of speaking her words for her, the wrongness of using this *I* that was hers
and not mine, this word that was not sufficiently capacious. (p. 185)

The interpreter-protagonist in Kitamura's story finds it difficult to maintain a
controlled position within the "alien I." As a result, she struggles to navigate
the porous boundary between the witness/victim and herself. She inadvertently
reveals her emotional stress through the trembling in her voice, which she
then self-consciously mentions to contrast with the "steady and solid and
strong" voice of the witness (p. 186). What bothers Kitamura's interpreter is
the interference of her own voice in the witness's oral account, a concern for
failing to alienate her personal "I" and thus weakening the narrative power of
the witness's "I." This further affirms the overwhelming task of speaking for
another person, with the interpreter wrestling with the intensity of her own
emotions that cannot be fully masked by the "alien I."

The intimacy of interpreting not only exists in a common but problematic
personal pronoun that disturbs the interpreter's emotional space but also
deepens through repeated face-to-face encounters in a shared space of
linguistic and physical proximity. In interpreted events where one or more
"foreign" languages are used, the level of linguistic intimacy increases
between the interpreter and the speaker/listener if they are among the few
people on-site who speak the same language. Spatially, when seated next to
the speaker at an in-person meeting, the interpreters' corporeal presence and
their vocal participation make the interaction not only an interlingual but also
an interpersonal one. Whispered interpreting or *chuchotage*, for instance,
creates a particular kind of intimate space where the interpreters are expected
to stay physically close to the listener and whisper the interpretation to their
ear.[4] Kitamura's fictional interpreter in *Intimacies* is drawn into these kinds of
interactions with a high-profile defendant accused of ethnic cleansing and
other crimes. The interpreter's visibility is maximized in these encounters,
with her voice, tone, body language, and even handwriting becoming the
subject of scrutiny. The complication of the interpersonal encounters outside
the formal conference setting of simultaneous interpreting adds yet another
layer to the intimacies she experiences.

In Kitamura's story, the interpreter-protagonist is requested by name to
work at legal counseling sessions and interpret for the defendant in the
consecutive and *chuchotage* modes after simultaneously interpreting the trial

---

[4] *Chuchotage* in the legal setting is the whispering mode of simultaneous interpreting
carried out by interpreters who are seated either behind or next to the person who
needs to hear the interpretation (Hale, 2015, p. 67).

proceedings in the booth for days. What puzzles the interpreter as she moves from the interpreter's booth to the meeting room is the double-binding situation of trust and visibility. Upon entering the room, she is greeted by the defendant, who has been charged with atrocious crimes. The man in question personally shows appreciation for her arrival in French, the language only the two of them can speak proficiently there. The interpreter then works in physical proximity to the accused, where she is "close enough to observe the texture of his skin" (p. 115). Their encounter involves both verbal and nonverbal exchanges: the accused nods at the interpreter, and she nods back; he shows his care for her, asking whether she is fine with the task; he also glances at her notepads, and they occasionally share a few comments on the interpreter's task (p. 120). These moments demonstrate how the intimacy of the encounter encroaches on the workplace of the interpreter, with herself not fully being aware of its risks and consequences. The relationship between the interpreter and the defendant here is affected by what is called "the glimmer of familiarity" —the close ties with the clients that professional interpreters tend to avoid so as not to compromise impartiality (Koskinen, 2020, p. 102).

The affective bonding between the protagonist and the accused over the progression of the trial after repeated personal contact takes a noticeable toll on the interpreter's emotional state. The protagonist is bothered by the intimate manners of the accused, who seemingly treats her as *his* interpreter. Her composure is disturbed by the defendant's non-verbal acknowledgment of her presence, as he would always look directly through the glass window of the booth and nod at her (p. 175). The accumulating familiarity in either the proximate or distanced interpreting mode makes it challenging for the interpreter to perform in a neutral or impartial manner. On the contrary, she notices how she is forced to take the man's perspective and, once again, gets lost in the "alien I," and feels "like being placed inside a body I had no desire to occupy" (p. 177). The occupancy metaphor amplifies the experience of interpreting as an intimate encounter and how it invades the interpreter's personal space and infringes on her right to work independently. The interpreter also realizes that her interpreting work functions as a buffer for the accused, who is bored by "the recitation of his own crimes" (p. 121); the presence of her voice creates a linguistically familiar and neutral space: "I was pure instrument, someone without will or judgment, a consciousness-free zone into which he could escape" (p. 121). In this context, the interpreter's self is highjacked by the defendant to serve as a talking companion and a moral vacuum. The instrumentalization of the interpreter's role demoralizes her work, leaving her in a state of subservience and uneasiness.

The implicated interpreter

Through the intimate encounters of her interpreter-protagonist, Kitamura revisits the tropes of interpreters' invisibility and neutrality and demonstrates that contradictions in such ethical expectations or codes may push the interpreter into volatile conditions. At the beginning of the novel, the interpreter-protagonist shares a story about her colleague Amina, an interpreter who is accredited for her professional manners but still struggles to control revealing her own emotions in the tones she uses while interpreting. When interpreting witness testimonies against the atrocious crimes, she finds herself sounding too emotional; when interpreting details of the accusations against the defendant, she notices an acerbic and even reproachful tone in her own voice (p. 23). What happens to Amina is not a singular case of fiction; it finds its resemblances in real-life accounts of interpreters who served at major historical events such as the Nuremberg trial and the International Criminal Tribunal for the Former Yugoslavia (ICTY):

> From the very beginning the interpreting staff at Nuremberg realized that the personality and voice of the interpreters were not to detract from the witnesses' and defendants' testimony. The listeners had to be unaware of the interpreters and accept their voices as original. This was not easy to achieve, though. Some interpreters colored the original version through vocal inflection or a particular rendering of the speech...Some interpreters were unemphatic and relaxed; others spoke in a rush, dramatically. (Gaiba, 1998, pp. 106-107)

> It is true that many ICTY interpreters have cried during testimony or been depressed thereafter. But so have the judges and lawyers. Because the stories they heard were harrowing, because the witnesses they observed were true to life, and because the interpretation was faithful. The Tribunal's interpreters are not afraid of letting their humanity show, echoing that of the speakers they interpret for. (Nikolić qtd. in Elias-Bursać, 2015, p. 52)

At the heart of Amina's spontaneous feelings, as well as with the Nuremberg interpreter's "interference" with the testimony and the ICTY interpreter's demonstration of "humanity," lies the jagged boundary between the interpreter's professional self and the personal self and the blurred lines between the voices, emotions, and intentions of the speaker and the interpreter.

The interpreters play a professional role, through which neutrality or impartiality are often taken as indicators of good performances of professionalism; the interpreters are also humans with their own personalities and emotions, and the prohibition or management of such traits requires affective (Koskinen, 2020, p.105) or emotional labor (Ayan, 2020, p.130), which is in itself an emotionally taxing task. The emotional toll on the interpreters has also been affirmed as a form of "ethical stress" that may ensue such psychological issues as vicarious trauma and burnout (Hubscher-Davidson, 2020, p. 424). Through Amina's emotional oscillation, Kitamura presents a pedagogical case about the uncertain zones the interpreters enter as they aim to abide by the professional codes while withholding their own feelings and struggling to do justice to others' words. Even though the "alien I" ostensibly allows the interpreter to flexibly shift between opposing positions or competing agendas, the interpreter's tones and emotions evince the non-erasability of the interpreter's personal "I" that is implicated in the process of legal justice.

During the portrayed court hearings, the nuanced shifts in Amina's tone were also detected by the accused, who cast his intimidating gaze to the interpreter's booth, as if accusing the interpreter of being disloyal. And, to his satisfaction, this nonverbal threat inflicts the interpreter's fear and disrupts the fluency of her delivery. The accused then retrieves his gaze and never looks back, leaving the interpreter in a strange sense of guilt (p. 25). Amina's story foreshadows what the interpreter-protagonist later experiences in the novel, as the emotional and ethical burden of interpreting also destabilizes her in the face of power and intimidation. As the interpreter-protagonist continues to interpret for the accused on trial, her personal morals keep rejecting the intimacies that bond them together, but her professional duty still pushes her to embody his perspective. The moral weight of the ongoing negotiation of distance and affinity leads to the onset of strong negative emotions, including repulsion and disgust (p. 178). At a final meeting after the Court rules to drop the criminal charges, the defendant takes the interpreter's lukewarm responses to his successful defense as a signal of her moral disapproval. He instantly breaks the previously cordial work relationship by initiating verbal aggression. "You sit there, so smug... But you are no better than me... there is nothing that separates you from me" (p. 212). The ethical implication of the interpreter in the trial, as the defendant declares, is threefold: her institutional role that aligns her with the procedural justice of the Court; her racial identity as Japanese/Japanese diaspora in relation to the country's history of war and violence; and her interpretation service as an integral part of his defense team that contributed to his exoneration. This imagined scenario of a highly personal insult targeting the interpreter corroborates and expands on what Kayoko Takeda describes as "interpreters' proximity to violence" (2021, p. 103), which entails the risks and dangers the interpreters are exposed to in war and conflict zones. For the interpreters in Kitamura's novel, the impact of such violence is manifested in the form of verbal attacks and emotional manipulation that the interpreter finds impossible to bear on her own.

In contrast to the extremity of workplace harassment the interpreter experiences, the professional guidelines she receives not only show a lack of a protection mechanism but also discourage her moral subjectivity. In another face-to-face encounter, the interpreter-protagonist is approached by Kees, a lawyer leading the defense team on the case. The man condescendingly draws a line between his "inured" status as an experienced lawyer and the interpreter's emotional volatility as an indicator of her professional incompetence (p. 118). "Inure" is a word that Kitamura's characters use to suggest how one may gradually get accustomed to a job, regardless of what ethical dilemmas the situation may present. One of the interpreter-protagonist's senior colleagues similarly advises her to adapt herself to the system: "You will get used to it. It becomes normal" (p. 174). In these cases, the act of getting inured suggests taking a neutral position as an employee embedded within the institution, where one is not obliged to make moral judgments other than just do the job. In her pedagogical work on ethics and morality in the context of translation, Mona Baker has criticized such a model of professionalism for not equipping translators and interpreters with sufficient toolkits to deal with the complexity of ethical issues (2018, p. 307). In addition, Baker casts doubt on the universal applicability of professional codes and highlights the responsibility of translators and interpreters to "question the code in order to avoid causing harm to others or perpetuating potential forms of injustice" (2018, p. 307). It is precisely due to the lack of preparation for the moral proximity of the interpreting job that the interpreter-protagonist in Kitamura's novel struggles to find an inner balance. The physical proximity of the interpreters to threats and manipulation means the harm and injustice caused by the rigid application of professional codes may affect not only others but also the interpreters themselves.

Toward the interpreter's autonomy

What the interpreter-protagonist discovers, as she has tried but failed to internalize the professional codes of the structured legal system, is a universal ethical quandary behind the seemingly smooth operation of the professional norms. She begins to see the "well-adjusted individuals," including the lawyers, her colleagues, and the defendant, as people living with "alarming fissures" (p. 187). Therefore, when her temporary contract with the interpretation section of the Court comes to an end, she declines the offer to become a permanent staff interpreter, a position she originally wanted. "I no longer believed that equanimity was either tenable or desirable. It corroded everything inside" (p. 218). The interpreter's decision to quit the job marks a breakaway from the manipulative power that shatters her sense of self and the neutral position that she finds impossible to sustain. The resignation can also be read as an act of self-intimacy where personal subjectivity overrides professional norms. In parallel with her career choice, the protagonist also moves out of her boyfriend's apartment, thus signaling her refusal to remain invisible and secondary in his life and the choice to temporarily step out of the intimate space. The decision to retreat from both environments that tie her down to a subservient position shows the emergence of the interpreter's autonomy.

In relation to the interpreter's awakening sense of self, an inter-semiotic translation is inserted into the plot of the novel, as the interpreter-protagonist sees the painting titled "Man Offering Money to a Young Woman" by Dutch artist Judith Leyster in the Mauritshuis Museum. The narrator's ekphrasis and critique of the painting give an allegorical representation of the interpreter's professional dilemma through the image of a seamstress who is approached by a man, with money in his right hand and left hand resting on her arms in an intimate manner.

> The young woman—girl, really—was working a piece of embroidery, some small domestic task that seemed of unlikely interest to the young man in his Cossack hat and tunic. He leered down at her, it was obviously not the task but rather the young girl herself who had caught his attention. She was in white, he was in black, the symbolism was clear enough but the exact nature of the encounter was opaque to me.
> (p. 127)

The subservient image of the woman, as she is placed in a sitting position lower than the standing man and being offered payment by the man with ambiguous and potentially sexual intentions, attracts the keen interest of Kitamura's narrator. She lingers at the painting for a long while and tries to interpret the "subtleties of force and resistance" in this man-woman relationship (p. 128). The narrator's encounter with this painting appears in the novel when she starts to question the function of her interpreting services as a moral vacuum for the defendant and her role in her boyfriend's life as an invisible sojourner. The interpreter mirrors her own situation in her reading of the painting, in which the seamstress is observed to be very focused on her work, and her meticulous labor remains unacknowledged other than the luring material benefits. The ethical dilemma for both this seamstress and the interpreter is to maintain "the perfect modesty" in a dire situation of "harassment and intimidation" (pp. 128-129). The indeterminacy of the seamstress in this painting unlocks multiple possibilities of her propensity to react to the intimate encounter mired in power imbalance and moral ambiguity: will she keep focusing on her work, or will she put down the cloth and accept the money?

The interpreter's final decision in the novel can thus be translated back to the painting as an alternative response of the seamstress: she might as well stop working on the piece and walk away from the scene. As the protagonist in Kitamura's novel puts an end to the unbearable intimacies of her interpreting job, she begins to develop more sustainable intimate relationships with herself and others. A critical event that sets the interpreter free is a phone call she made to her mother after leaving the Court, from which she is reminded that the city of the Hague is not a non-place for her but a place filled with intimate memories of her childhood and family life. At that moment, she regains an intimacy with the city and realizes that she is, after all, not a stranger. With a sense of belonging and connectivity restored, the interpreter gains her autonomy to decide whether she is to settle down with her lover in the city or move on to the next stop in her life. From there, the author provides an open ending that invites the reader to decide what will happen next.

Conclusion

The interpreters' participatory role and, more recently, their emotional engagement in interpreted events have been the central issues discussed among interpreting scholars (e.g., Wadensjö, 1998; Diriker, 2004; Maier, 2008; Hokkanen, 2017; Ayan, 2020). These studies have corroborated the implication of the interpreter's subjective self in interpreting-related social interactions and the interpreter's shifting positions between involvement/intervention and detachment/neutrality. Carol Maier (2008) employs the term "intervenient beings" (p. 2) to describe translators and interpreters, acknowledging them as individuals who may affect and be affected by their professional tasks. Maier, drawing on both fictional and non-fictional accounts of the interpreter's unpreparedness for "the emotional aspects of interpreting" (2008, p. 3), underscores a rift between ethical expectations and personal feelings. Kitamura's fictional work could also serve as a pedagogical text that foregrounds ethical issues in relation to the interpreters' emotional responses as a form of intervention. The fictional interpreter character in *Intimacies* not only performs her professional or institutional role but also is shown to live as a human being who thinks, feels, and changes. Therefore, her (in)visibility, neutrality, and mobility are constantly negotiated and re-negotiated through her self-reflection and social interactions.

Rosemary Arrojo (2010) asserts that literary texts with fictional translators and interpreters can inform both students learning the discourse of translation theory and non-specialists who might be used to criticizing or even condemning the translator's work (p. 54). To this end, Kitamura's text offers great insights for multiple audiences, including interpreting practitioners and readers from all walks of life, who are invited to follow the interpreter's first-person "I" and situate themselves in those intimate encounters and moral ambiguities. Kitamura's transfictional work also creatively weaves together the intrapersonal, intertextual, and intersemiotic threads about the professional self and private self, the translator and the text, and the interpreter and the message. These relational moments open the venue for further discussions about the ethical positionality of translators or interpreters who are implicated in the overwhelmingly intimate space of telling the stories of others while coping with the complexity of their own lives.

References

Arrojo, R. (2007). Fidelity and the gendered translation. *TTR*, *7*(2), 147–163. https://doi.org/10.7202/037184ar

Arrojo, R. (2010). Fictional texts as pedagogical tools. In C. Maier & F. Massardier-Kenney (Eds.), *Literature in translation: Teaching issues and reading practices*. Kent State University Press.

Arrojo, R. (2017). *Fictional translators: Rethinking translation through literature*. Routledge. https://doi.org/10.4324/9781315738727

Ayan, I. (2020). Re-thinking neutrality through emotional labour: The (in)visible work of conference interpreters. *TTR*, *33*(2), 125–146. https://doi.org/10.7202/1077714ar

Baer, B. (2005). Translating the transition: The translator-detective in post-Soviet fiction. *Linguistica Antverpiensia*, *4*, 243–54.

Baker, M. (2018). *In other words: A coursebook on translation* Third Edition. Routledge. https://doi.org/10.4324/9781315619187

Beebee, T. O. (1994). The fiction of translation: Abdelkebir Khatibi's "Love in Two Languages." *SubStance*, *23*(1), 63. https://doi.org/10.2307/3684793

Bielsa, E. (2016). *Cosmopolitanism and translation: Investigations into the experience of the foreign*. Routledge.

Borges, J. L. (1998). Pierre Menard: Author of the Quixote. In *Collected Fictions: Jorge Luis Borges* (A. Hurley, Trans.). (pp. 88–95). Penguin Books.

Cortázar, J. (1972). Carta a una señorita en París. In *Relatos* (pp. 9-19). Editorial Sudamericana Sociedad Anónima.

Cronin, M. (2002). The empire talks back: Orality, heteronomy, and the cultural turn in interpretation studies. In M. Tymoczko & E. Gentzler (Eds.), *Translation and power* (pp. 45–62). University of Massachusetts Press.

Cronin, M. (2009). *Translation goes to the movies*. Routledge. https://doi.org/10.4324/9780203890806

Delabastita, D., & Grutman, R. (2005). Introduction: Fictional representations of multilingualism and translation. *Linguistica Antverpiensia*, *4*, 11–35.

Diriker, E. (2004). *De-/re-contextualizing conference interpreting: interpreters in the ivory tower?* John Benjamins Publishing Company.

Elias-Bursać, E. (2015). *Translating evidence and interpreting testimony at a war crimes tribunal.* Palgrave Macmillan UK. https://doi.org/10.1057/97811 37332677

Gaiba, F. (1998). *The origins of simultaneous interpretation: The Nuremberg Trial.* University of Ottawa Press.

Guzmán, M. C. (2006). The spectrum of translation in Cortázar's "Letter to a Young Lady in Paris". *Íkala Revista de Lenguaje y Cultura, 11*(17), 75–86.

Hale, S. (2015). Community interpreting. In F. Pöchhacker (Ed.), *Routledge Encyclopedia of Interpreting Studies* (pp. 65–69). Routledge.

Hokkanen, S. (2017). Experiencing the interpreter's role: Emotions of involvement and detachment in simultaneous church interpreting. *Translation Spaces, 6*(1), 62–78. https://doi.org/10.1075/ts.6.1.04hok

Hubscher-Davidson, S. (2020). Ethical stress in translation and interpreting. In K. Koskinen & N. K. Pokorn (Eds.), *The Routledge Handbook of Translation and Ethics* (pp. 415–430). Routledge. https://doi.org/10.4324/978100312797 0-31

Inghilleri, M. (2012). *Interpreting justice: Ethics, politics and language.* Routledge.

Jansen, H. (2019). I'm a translator and I'm proud: How literary translators view authors and authorship. *Perspectives. Studies in Translation Theory and Practice, 27*(5), 675–688. https://doi.org/10.1080/0907676X.2018.1530268

Kaindl, K. (2014). Of dragons and translators: Foreignness as a principle of life. Yoko Tawada's 'St. George and the Translator'. In K. Kaindl & K. Spitzl (Eds.), *Transfiction: Research into the realities of translation fiction* (pp. 87–101). John Benjamins Publishing Company.

Kaindl, K. (2104). Going fictional! Translators and interpreters in literature and film: An introduction. In K. Kaindl, & K. Splitz (Eds.), *Transfiction: Research into the realities of translation fiction* (pp. 1-26). John Benjamins Publishing Company.

Kaindl, K., & Spitzl, K. (Eds.). (2014). *Transfiction: Research into the realities of translation fiction.* John Benjamins Publishing Company.

Kitamura, K. M. (2017). *A separation.* Riverhead Books.

Kitamura, K. M. (2021). *Intimacies.* Riverhead Books.

Koskinen, K. (2020). *Translation and affect: Essays on sticky affects and translational affective labour* (Vol. 152). John Benjamins Publishing Company. https://doi.org/10.1075/btl.152

Kurz, I. (2014). On the (in)fidelity of (fictional) interpreters. In K. Kaindl & K. Spitzl (Eds.), *Transfiction: Research into the realities of translation fiction* (pp. 205–220). John Benjamins Publishing Company.

Leal, A. (2023). Between omnipotence and humility: Scliar's fictional translator and Borges' Pierre Menard. In D. M. Spitzer & P. Oliveira (Eds.), *Transfiction and bordering approaches to theorizing translation: Essays in dialogue with the work of Rosemary Arrojo,* (pp. 41–53). Routledge.

Maier, C. (2008). The translator as an intervenient being. In J. Munday (Ed.), *Translation as intervention* (pp. 1–17). Continuum.

Miletich, M. (2022). Ways to (Dis)Appear: Dragomans committing suicide in stories by Julio Cortázar and Rodolfo Walsh. *Transletters. International Journal of Translation and Interpreting, 6,* 89–108.

Pagano, A. S. (2002). Translation as testimony: On official histories and subversive pedagogies in Cortázar. In M. Tymoczko & E. Gentzler (Eds.), *Translation and power* (pp. 80–98). University of Massachusetts Press.

Parkert, C. (2002). *Witness.* Oberon Books.

Pym, A. (2011). The translator as non-author, and I am sorry about that. In C. Buffagni, B. Garzelli, & S. Zanotti (Eds.), *The translator as author: Perspectives on literary translation* (pp. 31–43). Berlin: LIT Verlag.

Pym, A. (2012). *On translator ethics: Principles for mediation between cultures.* John Benjamins Publishing Company.

Scliar, M. (1995). Notas ao pé da página. In *Contos Reunidos* (pp. 371–75). Companhia das Letras.

Spitzl, K. (2014). Fiction as a catalyst. In K. Kaindl & K. Spitzl (Eds.), *Transfiction: Research into the realities of translation fiction* (pp. 363–368). John Benjamins Publishing Company.

Spivak, G. C. (2002). The politics of translation. In L. Venuti (Ed.), *The Translation Studies reader* Fourth Edition, pp. (320–338). Routledge.

Steiner, G. (1998). *After Babel: Aspects of language and translation.* Oxford University Press.

Strümper-Krobb, S. (2003). The translator in fiction. *Language and intercultural communication, 3*(2), 115–121. https://doi.org/10.1080/14708470308668095

Takeda, K. (2019). Mediating violence: Three film portrayals of interpreters' dilemmas as participants in conflict. In D. Abend-David (Ed.), *Representing translation: The representation of translation and translators in contemporary media* (pp. 45–67). Bloomsbury.

Takeda, K. (2021). *Interpreters and war crimes.* Routledge. https://doi.org/10.4324/9781003094982

Tawada, Y. (2007). St. George and the translator. In *Facing the Bridge* (M. Mitsutani Trans.). (pp. 176–186). New Directions Books.

Thiem, J. (1995). The translator as hero in postmodern fiction. *Translation and Literature, 4*(2), 207–218.

Valdeón, R. A. (2013). Doña Marina/La Malinche: A historiographical approach to the interpreter/traitor. *Target. International Journal of Translation Studies, 25*(2), 157–179. https://doi.org/10.1075/target.25.2.02val

Wadensjö, C. (1998). *Interpreting as interaction.* Routledge.

Wakabayashi, J. (2005). Representation of translators and translation in Japanese fiction. *Linguistica Antverpiensia, 4,* 155–69.

Walsh, R. (1981). Nota al pie. In *Rodolfo Walsh: Obra literaria completa* (pp. 419-446). Siglo XXI Editores S. A.

Wilson, R. (2011). Cultural mediation through translingual narrative. *Target. International Journal of Translation Studies, 23*(2), 235–250. https://doi.org/10.1075/target.23.2.05wil

Chapter 5

Translator (In)Visibility in Rodolfo Walsh's "La aventura de las pruebas de imprenta"

Marko Miletich

SUNY Buffalo State University

Abstract: Rodolfo Walsh's "La aventura de las pruebas de imprenta" [The Adventure of the Printing Proofs] begins with the death of a translator/editor and the subsequent investigation to untangle the mysterious circumstances surrounding this fatality. The primary pieces of evidence are the marks left behind in the translator/editor's printing proofs, which provide clues as to the cause of his demise. Efforts to establish whether the translator's death was an accident, suicide, or murder depend on the very visibility of these types of wordsmiths. Thus, the story, thorough its astute detective à la Sherlock Holmes, calls attention to the traces left behind by the translator/editor and his inescapable presence, even after he has passed on. This fascinating whodunnit offers a glimpse of the publishing world as it sheds light on the visibility of translators and editors. In addition, Walsh's story serves to illustrate parallels between the work of translators and detectives.

Keywords: detective, translator/editor, (in)visibility, transfiction, Walsh

***

But I have been told that you understand everything, and you can solve
difficult problems. Now then, if you can read this writing and tell me
what it means, you will become the third most powerful man
in my kingdom. You will wear royal purple robes
and have a gold chain around your neck.

(Daniel: 5:13 Contemporary English Version)

Introduction

"La aventura de las pruebas de imprenta" [The Adventure of the Printing Proofs][1] by Rodolfo Jorge Walsh introduces us to a murder scene: a translator/editor is found dead in a closed room, with a bullet wound to his right eye. An investigation ensues to unravel the mystery of this loss of life. The story is narrated in the third person by an extradiegetic narrator and consists of nine chapters and an appendix. It revolves around the mysterious death of a translator, Raimundo Morel, who works for Editorial Corsario [Corsair Publishing House] and is translating a collection of works by Oliver Wendell Holmes (the use of the last name Holmes is one of several nods to Sir Arthur Conan Doyle's famous detective).[2] Printing proofs left behind by the deceased translator become the centerpiece of the story as a police investigator and an editor/amateur detective, Daniel Hernández (who shares his first name with the biblical prophet) are called to the scene. It falls upon the editor to decipher the mystery of Morel's death.

Rodolfo Jorge Walsh was an Argentine writer and journalist of Irish descent born in 1927 in the province of Río Negro, Argentina. In 1944, Walsh began working as an editor/proofreader at the publishing house Hachette in Buenos Aires, where he also translated detective fiction. Not surprisingly, Walsh's own experiences as an editor and translator are often reflected in his work. In fact, Rodolfo Walsh published the first Argentine anthology of its kind: *Diez cuentos policiales argentinos* [Ten Argentine Detective Stories] (1953). In his introduction to the book, Walsh (pp. 6-8) explains that the first book of detective stories, entitled *Seis problemas para don Isidro Parodi* [Six Problems for Don Isidro Parodi], was first published in 1942 by Jorge Luis Borges and Adolfo Bioy Casares under the joint pseudonym H. Bustos Domecq.[3] In 1953, he published a collection of short stories entitled *Variaciones en rojo* [Variations in Red]. The collection contains three detective stories: "La aventura de las pruebas de imprenta" [The Adventure of the Printing Proofs], "Variaciones en rojo" [Variations in Red] and "Asesinato a distancia" [Murder

---

[1] Printing proofs are often called "galleys."
[2] Oliver Wendell Holmes, Sr. (August 29, 1809 - October 7, 1894) was an American physician, poet, professor, lecturer, and author based in Boston. His most famous prose works are the "Breakfast-Table" series, which began with *The Autocrat at the Breakfast-Table* (1858). He then published *The Professor at the Breakfast-Table* (1859), *The Poet at the Breakfast-Table* (1872), and *Over the Teacups* (1890). In addition, he also wrote three novels: *Elsie Venner* (1861), *The Guardian Angel* (1867), and *A Mortal Antipathy* (1885).
[3] The pseudonym is a combination of names from both authors. Bustos was a great-grandfather of Borges, and Domecq was an ancestor of Bioy Casares (Bird, 2007, p.73). The *H* stands for Honorio.

from a Distance].[4] Walsh also published other detective stories whose protagonist is a retired detective by the name of Comisario [Police Chief] Laurenzi. The stories are entitled "Los casos del comisario Laurenzi" [Police Chief Laurenzi's Cases] and they appear in the short story collection *La máquina del bien y el mal* [The Good and Evil Machine] (1992). Walsh is best known for *Operación masacre* [Operation Massacre], a work of investigative journalism first published in 1957. Walsh was the founder of the *Prensa Latina* news agency and edited several political newspapers. He also wrote "Carta abierta de un escritor a la Junta Militar" [Open Letter from a Writer to the Military Junta] (1977). In this letter, the writer disclosed the regime's atrocities and called for accountability and justice. Shortly after the publication of that letter, he was "disappeared" and assassinated by the military dictatorship. His complete works were published posthumously in Mexico in 1981.

This chapter analyzes the way in which Rodolfo Walsh's transfictional story[5] "La aventura de las pruebas de imprenta" provides a "visible" tour of the publishing industry and its process. The story also serves as a vehicle to "detect" the many ways in which translators and editors are inevitably visible through their textual choices, translatorial decisions, and proofreading marks. In addition, the story showcases the similarities between the role of the detective and that of the translator.

Translators as Word Sleuths

There is a palpable connection between translators and detectives. Both look for clues to provide a result that is satisfactory, either to society (in the case of detectives) as a criminal is put away or to readers (in the case of translators) as they are granted access to a foreign text. Both professionals are able to uncover information that would otherwise be inaccessible to their clientele

---

[4] These stories are included in *Rodolfo Walsh: Obra literaria completa* [Rodolfo Walsh: The Complete Literary Works] (1981). These three stories also feature the editor/ detective Daniel Hernández. "Asesinato a distancia" [Murder from a Distance], like "La aventura de las pruebas de imprenta" also deals with the circumstance of a possible accident, suicide, or murder. Several of Walsh's detective stories became part of a television series entitled *Variaciones Walsh,* broadcasted by TV Pública in Argentina (Cruz et al., 2015). The series was based on twelve police stories by Rodolfo Walsh, adapted by Esther Feldman and Alejandro Maci. It premiered on October 8, 2015, and it was composed of 13 episodes. The first episode was "La aventura de las pruebas de imprenta" (Feldman & Maci, 2015).

[5] As discussed throughout this volume the term, transfiction describes fiction that focuses on translation, translators, or interpreters as part of its narrative. Transfictional is the adjective used to describe these types of stories.

without their assistance. Sabine Strümper-Krobb (2014) explains in detail the relationship between these two professions:

> There are several parallels between translation and crime detection. Translators are expected first to identify the function and meaning of particular elements of a text in order to reconstruct them as truthfully as possible in a different language, so that the reader is able to understand them appropriately. Similarly, a detective needs to collect evidence in a criminal case before he or she is able to reconstruct the crime in such a way that the reconstructed version corresponds to the actual course of events. (p. 130)

Strümper-Krobb goes on to discuss the reason why writers of crime fiction are interested in characters who are translators and interpreters since these language professionals can:

> not only drive forward a plot involving mystery and suspense, but also often contribute significantly to a discourse about the possibility of unambiguous truths, of clear distinctions between original and copy, reality, and fiction. It is thus not surprising that the writers of crime fiction have taken such an interest in translator figures and in the theme of translation. (2014, p. 131)

Walsh's transfictional tale provides another nod to Sir Arthur Conan Doyle's famous detective, Sherlock Holmes (the first one being Walsh's selection of the author being translated by Morel, Oliver Wendell Holmes). It appears when Hernández is talking to his colleague, Aurelio Rodríguez, who is helping in the investigation and who is introduced as an "unpredictable and ephemeral Watson" (35).[6] The fact that Rodríguez does not notice the lack of clues (some of Morel's corrections on the printing proofs are more legible than others) leads the main character to cite one of the stories that features Sherlock Holmes, "The Silver Blaze." Rodríguez, like Watson, does not understand what his colleague Hernández sees:

> Have you forgotten the classics? The curious incident of the dog was that it had not barked at night. And the curious incident of these two or three corrections is that they are well done, they are well written in

---

[6] *"… imprevisible y efímero Watson".*

perfect handwriting, in the authentic handwriting of Morel. Do you understand now? (35)[7]

Another parallel that can be drawn between translators and detectives is the fact that they both expose the existence of something that is not perceptible. Detectives follow a path of discovery and inquiry to obtain specific information. Likewise, translators conduct research (also through discovery and inquiry) in foreign languages and investigate morphosyntactic, semantic, and pragmatic issues to provide textual information and accomplish their tasks. Another similarity between translators and detectives lies in the fact that detective stories are "based on a triad of characters: criminal-detective-victim" (Castellino, 1999, p. 91). Thus, someone commits a crime, someone is harmed in some way, and someone investigates to uncover the perpetrator. A translator's work is based on similar triads. There is the *source text-translation-target text* triad; a foreign text is written in a particular language, the text is read, understood, and transformed, and then the text is rewritten into a different language. There is also the *author-translator-reader* triad; someone writes in one language, someone rewrites that person's writing into another language, and someone reads the transformed source text as the target text. Additionally, detectives must get into a culprit's mind to understand them and solve a crime, while translators get into the mind of an author to understand them and re-create the author's ideas in a different language. Detectives make visible the invisible in order to solve a crime; translators make visible the invisible in order to provide some readers (those who read the target language, but not the source language) with otherwise inaccessible stories and ideas.

Barbara Wilson (pen name of Barbara Sjoholm), a contemporary award-winning translator from Danish and Norwegian and author of many travel books, memoirs, and biographies, combines the roles of translators and detectives in her work. Many of her fictional writings include the translator and amateur sleuth Cassandra Reilly, a lesbian translator and part-time detective who travels around the globe to solve inexplicable mysteries. In her most famous novel, *Gaudí Afternoon* (1990), Cassandra is hired to translate a novel by the "new female version of Gabriel García Márquez," but a new investigative mission interrupts her translation work: tracking down a friend's ex-husband. Wilson also published a collection of short stories entitled *The*

---

[7] "—*Ha olvidado los clásicos? —insistió Daniel—. El curioso incidente del perro era que no había ladrado de noche. Y el curioso incidente de estas dos o tres correcciones es que están bien hechas, están bien escritas con una letra perfecta, con la letra auténtica de Raimundo Morel. ¿Comprende ahora?"*

Death of a Much-Travelled Woman and Other Adventures with Cassandra Reilly (1998). Many of the pieces in this collection are basically detective stories, but there is one where both professions converge: in "Mi novelista" (Wilson, 1998, pp. 195-215),[8] Cassandra Reilly pseudo-translates a yet-unpublished work by a made-up author, Elvira Montalbán. After the success of Cassandra's translation, a woman claiming to be Elvira Montalbán writes the book that Cassandra Reilly has been pretending to translate. Cassandra Reilly uses her detective skills to expose the writer, who claims to be the author of her fictitious translation.

Another contemporary author who utilizes language professionals is Anthony Horowitz. His novel *Magpie Murders: A Novel* (2017) utilizes a novel-within-a-novel framework. One story is set in 1950s Saxby-on-Avon (England), where fictional detective Atticus Pünd investigates a murder. The other is set in modern-day London and involves an editor, Susan Ryeland, who discovers while reading a manuscript of a novel she is editing, that the final chapter is missing. She then sets out to solve the mystery of the death of the writer she is editing.[9]

Similarities between detectives and translators have been discussed, but it is worth repeating. Detective work and translation are intellectual endeavors that require a great deal of careful observation (mostly of physical clues for the detective and of textual clues for the translator) and a way to make visible what may otherwise be invisible to others. The way in which the editor, Hernández, unravels the mystery provides a comparison with the task of translators/editors and detectives. Both need investigative skills: detectives solve the mystery of a crime, and translators/editors solve the mystery of textual meaning to accomplish their translatorial activities. If a detective is often referred to as a "private eye" who needs this particular organ to carry out his/her profession, a translator could then be considered a "hermeneutical eye" who utilizes the same organ to see and then interpret, understand, and communicate an alterity.[10]

Rodolfo Walsh's word sleuths (both translator and editor) showcase the tightrope that translators tread between visibility and invisibility.

---

[8] The title of the story "*Mi novelista*" [My Novelist] appears in Spanish in the English text.

[9] The book has been made into a television series by American broadcaster Public Broadcasting Service (PBS) and has recently been shown in the United States (Cattaneo et al., 2022).

[10] Hermeneutics is also associated to the Greek god Hermes, who served as a messenger facilitating/transmitting messages between gods and mortals. Incidentally, together with Jerome, Hermes is one of the patrons of translation/interpreting.

Visibility

"La aventura de las pruebas de imprenta" opens with an epigraph from the Book of Daniel (verses 13-16) (1995, pp. 1044-1045) reproduced at the beginning of this chapter. The apposite quotation describes a mysterious message that appears on a wall while a king is giving a great banquet. All the king's wise men (enchanters, astrologers, and diviners) are summoned but are unable to tell the king what the mysterious words mean. Daniel–a subject who can interpret dreams, explain riddles, and unravel difficult problems–is brought to the king to decipher the message: the king's reign will soon come to an end and his kingdom is to be divided between two different tribes. Quite tellingly, it takes an interpreter of written signs to "translate" the ominous message. The story's epigraph immediately introduces a visible interpreter (translator) of a written message. Likewise, mysterious markings appear in Walsh's story (in the form of proofreading/editing marks), and someone is needed to interpret them. The task of deciphering these markings and relating the events that led to the fictional translator's death falls on an editor/ proofreader. It is not by chance that Walsh picked a biblical passage as his epigraph for this story since it introduces the topic of translation from the very start. The passage is, indeed, the translation of an ancient Biblical text, which Walsh cleverly uses to open a story that features translation.

Walsh's story begins by providing a detailed description of a publishing company named *Corsario* [Corsair], housed in the upper level of the building that also contains a bookstore owned by the same publishing company. Readers are immediately introduced to the publishing world and the way in which manuscripts are received and evaluated (pp. 11-12).[11] It is an astute way to introduce (and make visible) an environment that may not be familiar to people outside the field. Editing is also showcased through the omniscient narrator's description of the editing department, where "silent and engrossed proofreaders correct originals and proofs" (p. 12).[12] Later, a character is shown handling "the long print proofs" (p. 14). Additionally, Walsh presents the scene for a portion of the translation process with proofreading/editing marks clearly displayed on a page (p. 19).[13] The short story includes a reproduction

---

[11] Henceforth, page numbers following references and quotations from "La aventura de las pruebas de imprenta" indicate the page number in the Spanish text in Walsh (1981b) in References.

[12] "*... revisores silenciosos y absortos corrigen originales y las pruebas de imprenta*". All quotations in English from "La aventura de las pruebas de imprenta" are from my unpublished translations of the Spanish text.

[13] There are three reproductions of translations with proofreading/editing marks: Figure I (p. 19), Figure II (p. 36), and Figure III (p. 56). Due to space limitations, only the translation featured in Figure I will be discussed here.

of Morel's translation of the first three paragraphs of Oliver Wendell Holme's *The Poet at the Breakfast-Table* (1872). The story also provides readers with explanations for some of the proofreading symbols used in publishing, and shown in the reproduction of Morel's translation, thus making these marks and the proofreading/editing process visible: "The sign similar to the letter *fi* is called *deleatur* or simply 'dele'; it indicates that a word, letter, etc. should be deleted. The sign # indicates: 'separate'" (p. 18).[14] Walsh has exhibited visibly to the readers the way corrections/editions are used in proofing and integrated them as an important part of the plot, thus enabling them to visualize important aspects of the translation and publishing world.

The fictional translator is also shown debating his translatorial decisions:

> Morel showed some concern about some details of the version: he had not yet decided whether to translate directly the poems inserted in the text or whether it was preferable to include the original version and translate it in a footnote. He was also concerned about the marked localism of some of the allusions. These characteristics, in Daniel's opinion, were the reason why no one had yet translated Holmes. (p. 14)[15]

Walsh not only makes the translator visible but also showcases the decision-making process that all translators confront. This paragraph alone could serve to encourage discussion regarding several issues dear to translation studies: the translation of poetry (whether to translate a poem or include the original in the text), the use of footnotes (to include the translation of a foreign text), the intricacies of certain texts (how to translate words and phrases peculiar to one locality), and author selection (reasons why certain authors' works may not be selected for translation).

Morel, Walsh's fictional translator, decides "to tackle the translation into Spanish of perhaps the only one of the North American classics completely ignored in our language" (p. 13).[16] A work is made "visible" in a different cultural and linguistic context through the fictional translator. Similarly, real translators' choices and actions brought into view many twentieth-century

---

[14] "*El signo semejante a una letra fi se llama deleatur o simplemente 'dele'; indica que debe suprimirse una palabra, letra, etc. El signo # indica: 'separar'*".

[15] "*Morel demostró cierta inquietud por algunos detalles de la versión: aún no había resuelto si convenía traducir directamente los poemas intercalados en el texto, o si era preferible incluir la versión original y traducirla en nota al pie. Lo inquietaba, además, el marcado localismo de algunas alusiones. Esas características, a juicio de Daniel, eran el motivo por el cual aún nadie había traducido a Holmes*".

[16] "*... abordar la traducción al castellano del único quizá de los clásicos norteamericanos completamente ignorado en nuestra lengua...*"

Latin American writers for English language readers in the United States. It was thanks to translators such as Gregory Rabassa, who worked closely with the Center for Inter-American Relations in New York that this became possible.[17] As Rabassa (2005) describes in his book *If This Be Treason: Translation and Its Discontents*, the Center became in the 1960s "the organization most responsible for the dissemination in the United States of the works of the Latin American 'Boom'" (p. 75). In fact, Rabassa "played a key role in the internationalization of Latin American literature, which turned out to be a significant element in the formation of its canon and the configuration of its global image" (Guzmán, 2013, p. 92). Much like Rabassa, the dead translator in Walsh's story, Morel, intervenes in helping to disseminate a literary text written in a different language by making it available to a particular audience (in Walsh's story a fictional Spanish-speaking audience).

Even before readers start to read the story, they are introduced to a translation of a Biblical text; thus, this is an act of translation that makes visible the role of a translator (an interpreter of a written text). A translation's path toward final publication is shown to provide a bird's eye view of the publishing world and the role of the translator in the publishing process. Traditionally, the translator's labor is effaced (at times even self-effaced). In this transfictional story, however, the translator is prominently displayed as an intellectual and a valuable, contributing member of society which makes visible a literary otherness. This story makes evident some of the translatorial decisions regularly taken by translators, and thus serves to enlighten readers of the intricacies of the translator's task.

Walsh's fictional translator in "*La aventura de las pruebas de imprenta*" starts off as a very visible character. The character is portrayed as an intellectual and sophisticated (visible) member of society, described as a "Harvard graduate [whose] critical appraisal of authors as disparate as Whitman, Emily Dickinson, and Stephen Crane had attracted profound attention" (p. 13).[18] He is, however, "invisibilized" through his death, as explored in the next section.

---

[17] The translation program of the Center for Inter-American Relations was based in New York City. It worked closely with a translation subsidy program administered by the Association of American University Presses, which was founded by Rockefeller philanthropies. The goals of the Center were to promote cross-cultural understanding. Additionally, it was intended to further US foreign policy interests in the Americas during the 1960s, taking into account the rise of Castro and the Cuban Revolution (Lowe & Fitz, 2007, p. xiii).

[18] "*Egresado de Harvard, su valoración crítica de autores tan dispares como Whitman, Emily Dickinson y Stephen Crane había llamado profundamente la atención*".

Invisibility

Soon after the story begins, a translator, Morel, is found dead. The use of death in literature is a recurrent trope and is "not merely preoccupied with the painful scene of dying or individual loss, but the concept of death can be understood more widely as a site of many projections and fantasies and as a metaphor of many social issues" (Hakola & Kivistö, 2014, p. viii). In Walsh's story the translator's death could be read as projected invisibility since death can be considered "a veritable change in state, a transformation from one kind of being to another kind of (non)being" (Hakola & Kivistö, 2014, p. x). The death of this fictional translator, then, creates an aura of invisibility–a topic that is often discussed in translation studies (as seen in discussions regarding the prominence of the author over the translator, a translator's name not displayed in a translated text, and a translatorial strategy utilized that effaces the translator).

Traditionally, the very act of translation provides a more obvious view of the author over the translator. Authors are dominant over translators who "remain silent, hiding the texts' foreignness" (Coldiron, 2012, p. 190). As far as invisibility is concerned, much is owed to discussions generated by Lawrence Venuti. Venuti's *The Translator' Invisibility: A History of Translation* (1995) argues that a translator's inconspicuousness is due to the status of a translator as reproducer of a text and an ambiguous legal status reinforced by the marketing, the reading, and evaluating of translations; the scarcity of texts to be translated into English from other languages; and the production of fluent target texts that tend to obscure the presence of the translator (pp. 1-10 and sic passim). Venuti (1995), following ideas first proposed by Friedrich Schleiermacher (1813),[19] uses the terms *domesticating* (producing a fluent, idiomatic translation following the culture of the language of that target text) and *foreignizing* (producing a less fluent, idiomatic translation which includes noticeable traces of the source text via word choices and/or syntax) (pp. 1-10 and sic passim). Venuti notes that reader expectations influence market forces and publisher's decisions to privilege "domestication" of foreign texts, thereby seeming to mitigate evidence of their foreign origins.

The translator's labor, then, is effaced "metaphorically as it submits to the reigning demands for fluency and readability in the target language" (Milkova, 2016, p. 166). Morel, the fictional translator in Walsh's story, is visible through his commentaries on the translatorial task (from p. 14 of the short story as previously discussed); nevertheless, the performance of his

---

[19] Schleiermacher proposes two different ways to translate: bringing the reader to the foreign text versus bringing the foreign text to the reader.

task creates an atmosphere of invisibility, which can be ascertained through his editing. Morel replaces the way he first translated words through his editing changes to produce a more readable idiomatic Spanish, which shows a tendency to use a "domesticating" approach to translation. [20] An approach that, following Venuti's theory, is a way to erase (make invisible) the otherness of the source text.

For example, "rather odd," was first translated as *sin duda* [without a doubt]. S*in duda* is already an idiomatic translation of English since the Spanish could have used *bastante raro, bastante extraño*. *Sin duda* is crossed out and replaced by *indudablemente* [undoubtedly], an even more idiomatic expression. *I have as many bound volumes of notions of one kind and another in my head*, was first translated as *tengo en la cabeza tantos volúmenes encuadernados de ideas de una y otra clase*, which is a very literal translation. The English phrase *have... in my head*, was first translated as *tengo en la cabeza* which again is a literal translation and closer syntactically to the English text. The word *tengo* is changed to *llevo* and the phrase becomes *llevo en la cabeza* [I carry in my head], which uses a more idiomatic way of expressing that idea. The translator translated *the matter in question* as *el asunto que se trata* [the matter at hand] while *el asunto en cuestión* [the matter in question] utilizing the cognate *cuestión*, was available. All these subtle changes suggest an inclination towards a "domesticating" strategy and an effort to achieve invisibility.

Apart from the brief encounter at the beginning of the story, the translator remains unseen. As he leaves the company of his colleague Hernández, he becomes undistinguishable (invisible) among the crowds: "They walked along Avenida de Mayo, and when they reached the corner of Piedras they separated. Morel continued along the avenue, stumbling through the river of passers-by" (p. 14).[21] Apart from Hernández, no one mentions seeing the translator. The translator's wife, Alberta Morel, claims to have seen him, but that is later determined to be untrue: "Alberta Morel had lied" (p. 59).[22]

Another "invisible" translator is featured in a different transfictional story by Walsh, entitled "Nota al pie" [Footnote].[23] That story starts with the image of a dead translator covered by a sheet. The translator is made invisible by physically concealing his body. Similarly, the translator's dead body in "La

---

[20] All these editing changes appear in Figure 1, p, 19 in the short story. The English text referenced in the story comes from "The Poet at the Breakfast-Table." It appears in Holmes (1872, p.1).

[21] "*Caminaron por la Avenida de Mayo, y al llegar a la esquina de Piedras se separaron. Morel siguió por la avenida tropezando por el río de transeúntes.*"

[22] "*...Alberta Morel había mentido*".

[23] For additional analysis of this story see Arrojo (2018a, pp. 34-46) and Miletich (2022).

aventura de las pruebas de imprenta" is at first invisible since no one–apart from Hernández–had seen him, and the door of the translator's office space, where Morel's body was found, was closed: "the studio door remained closed" (p. 15).[24] Another similarity between the two texts is that in "Nota al pie," the translator becomes visible by the constantly increasing length of footnotes in the story until the footnotes end up completely displacing the main text. Likewise, "La aventura de las pruebas de imprenta" utilizes proofreading/editing marks to make visible the reasons for Morel's sad ending.

The death of the fictional translator appears to render him invisible. The visible proofreading/editing marks left behind, however, demonstrate that the translator's visibility, through their work, endures beyond the act of translation and even beyond the translator's existence. Those visible marks (reproduced in the text by Walsh), are used to solve the mystery of the translator's death and show the movements of the deceased translator (apparently invisible through death), which brings him back to the world of living.

Upon returning home, Morel's wife, Alberta Morel, discovers her husband dead at his desk. At first glance, the death appears to be a suicide or an accident since Morel is found alone in a closed room, "invisible" from the outside, with a gunshot through his eye and a gun near his body. Interestingly, the translator is shot through the eye, the organ of sight that is indispensable to perform the task of translation to make a text "visible." It is through the eye that the mystery of Morel's death is solved, and it is through what others cannot see that a final interpretation of events (an interpretation similar to translating a textual otherness) can be discerned. The eye is the organ used for vision, and in Walsh's story in particular, the organ used by Morel to perform his job and also the main organ used for detective work. As the fictional editor scrutinizes the visible marks, readers are invited to clearly follow the developments of the story. These very marks reveal, through the astute observations of an editor/detective, how this fictional translator met his demise.

Accident, Suicide, or Murder?

An experienced police chief, Jiménez, starts the investigation and gathers witnesses at the scene, and different theories emerge. The chief soon believes he has solved the case, but Hernández, the editor/proofreader and the dead translator's colleague, is set to unravel the truth behind Morel's mysterious death by looking at the "visible" edited printing proofs that the translator has left behind. Hernández, who shares his name with the biblical Daniel, also shares "the prophet's ability to unravel the meaning of a scripture, an ability

---

[24] "*La puerta del estudio seguía cerrada*".

that Hernández demonstrates in his dual role as proofreader and amateur detective in the story" (Fernández Vega, 1997, p. 66, my translation).[25] The proofreader/editor possesses the ability to read (and see) what others cannot and make visible a message that was hidden and unreachable. This ability can be compared to the task of everyday translators as they read a source text (which is unreadable and with meaning invisible to many) to (re)create a target text. It is worth noting that Hernández is described as near-sighted (p. 12); he, nevertheless, can see more than others with perfect vision.

The death of the fictional translator may be due to three possible causes: accident, suicide, or murder. All of them are examined by the police chief, an insurance agent named Alvarado, and Hernández–the coworker of the deceased translator Morel.

An accident seems probable since a gun belonging to Morel was found next to the translator. In addition, there was a gun-cleaning solution on the table in the room where the body was found. It seemed plausible that Morel was cleaning the gun when he looked into the barrel and, unaware there was a bullet in the chamber, accidentally shot himself.

There are, however, reasons to believe it was a suicide. Raimundo's financial resources had diminished considerably since he spent most of his money on trips abroad and on books. Furthermore, he was recently denied a life insurance policy after a medical exam revealed he suffered a heart condition and was referred to a specialist. Nevertheless, no gunpowder was found in the hands of the deceased, and he left no suicide note.[26]

Murder, however, could also be the cause of the translator's death. The printing proofs found next to the deceased with their apparently illegible scribbles are first dismissed as the work of someone under the influence of alcohol since a bottle of whisky was found next to the translator's body. However, these seemingly insignificant proofs are, in fact, indispensable to

---

[25] "*La habilidad del profeta para desentrañar el sentido de unas escrituras, habilidad que Daniel Hernández pone de manifiesto en su doble papel de corrector de pruebas y detective aficionado en el cuento*".

[26] Both explanations, accident and suicide, undervalue (invisibilize) the translator as a person. An accident labels someone as careless and inept at a particular task. Suicide makes an individual seem unwell and unable to cope with the challenges of life. Accidents and suicides are created through an internal agent (self) while murder reflects the action of an external agent (another person or persons). Both accidental death and suicide can be perceived as less visible than murder, since in both cases investigations are usually completed quickly. Murder, on the other hand, demands a higher visibility since a longer exploration of a particular case must be conducted to determine how a crime was committed, and especially to identify the perpetrator.

solve the mystery of the fictional translator's death. In addition, the deceased translator "was editing his own translation" (60).[27] What the clever detective/editor does is give visibility to the editing/proofreading professions, which are often obscured to the point of receiving virtually no recognition. Editors and proofreaders are often even more invisible than translators. As Karen Shashok reminds us, "the role of the author's editor is rarely acknowledged in print" (2001, p. 113). Similar to translators who reword a text in a different language, editors reword a text to "either correct it or improve it" (Mossop, 2001, p. 223). In our story, the translator edits himself utilizing visible marks while a second editor/proofreader, Hernández, interprets those marks. It is the inevitable (and visible) trace left in the printing proofs that can serve to bring to light the perpetrator of a crime and the deceased translator himself since at least the last days of his life are examined through visible clues.

Hernández, the observant editor/proofreader, goes on to state, "These proofs speak" (60).[28] The proofs are the visible presence of the now defunct (invisible) translator. Walsh includes the corrections made by Morel in the story not only to have them visibly accessible but also to provide readers with the "sensation of being an active reader and participating in the solution of the mystery" (Gamerro, 2012, p. 4, my translation).[29]

The police chief observes what seems to him illegible handwritten corrections produced by an inebriated or emotionally unstable man (19). The prolonged handwritten letters and the misplaced dots over the *i*'s confirm the chief's suspicion. Some marks seemed excessively prolonged, and others almost atrophied. Some corrections, however, seem much more legible. The very irregular marks, however, will eventually serve to solve the mystery of the translator's death; Hernández asserts that the printing proofs reflect the translator's movement as he travelled by train to confront his wife's lover, Anselmo Benavídez. It seems that Morel's wife Alberta and her lover had planned the "accident" since she discovered that her husband was going to die from an incurable disease. They need the translator's death to appear as an accident to collect on their accidental death insurance. She provided her lover the keys to the house to stage the accident. Apparently, the deceased translator had recently discovered his wife's infidelity and had decided to confront her lover, who lives in La Plata–a short train ride from Morel's home in the city of Buenos Aires.[30]

---

[27] "*Morel estaba corrigiendo su propia traducción*".
[28] "*Estas pruebas hablan*".
[29] "*La sensación de ser un lector activo y de participar en la solución del misterio...*"
[30] In the story, train schedules are reproduced on pages 61 and 64. The appendix also details Morel's movements the evening before his death.

There are differences between the corrections in that some seem to be written legibly while others seem less legible; these differences are due to Morel working while traveling on a moving train. Our amateur detective believes that the visible marks leave a chronological table of his trip. Much like the biblical Daniel of the past, our amateur detective can decipher what others cannot; thus, the inconsistency in writing reflects a presence that can only be seen by the expert eyes of a careful reader. Daniel, the experienced editor, goes on to discuss the need to read differently: "read slowly... the purpose of reading the proofs is to discover the typos, the mistakes in construction, the deficiencies in the translation. This requires a slow, syllabic reading" (56).[31] He then adds, "But experienced proofreaders are always slow and careful" (57).[32]

The visible marks left on a printing proof, as illustrated in the story, serve to demonstrate that the task of the editor/proofreader is to detect and mark errors. Walsh, who worked as an editor and proofreader himself, educates readers on the necessary skills needed to be an editor:

Observation, meticulousness, imagination (so necessary, e.g., to interpret certain translations or original works), and above all, that rare ability to be simultaneously situated on different planes, which the experienced editor exercises when he pays attention, in the reading, to the typographical cleanliness, the sense, the goodness of the syntax and the fidelity of the version. (1985, p. 7, my translation)[33]

Editor's skills are very similar to those used by translators who must also read very carefully and write well to uncover a text in another language–skills that are also used by detectives in their jobs.

Conclusion

The transfictional story examined here, along with fictional texts focusing on issues related to translation, may serve as an introduction to the complex issues surrounding the translatorial task. Rosemary Arrojo points out that in contrast to more erudite scholarly writings, "fictional texts focusing on issues of translation, authorship, and reading can provide a more nuanced frame of

---

[31] *"...leer despacio... el fin de la lectura de las pruebas es descubrir las erratas, las faltas de construcción, las deficiencias de la traducción, Eso obliga a una lectura lenta, silabeada."*
[32] *"Pero los correctores experimentados son siempre lentos y cuidadosos".*
[33] *"La observación, la minuciosidad, la fantasía (tan necesaria, vgr., Para interpretar ciertas traducciones u obras originales), y sobre todo esa rara capacidad para situarse simultáneamente en planos distintos, que ejerce el corrector avezado cuando va atendiendo, en la lectura, a la limpieza tipográfica, al sentido, a la bondad de la sintaxis y a la fidelidad de la versión".*

reference" (2018b, p. 1). Walsh's crafty whodunnit brings up several issues often discussed in translation studies, such as the selection of authors to be translated, translatorial decisions, editing and proofreading, the publishing process, domesticating and foreignizing, and, of course, visibility versus invisibility.

Throughout this chapter, a correlation has been made between the (in)visibility of the fictional translator and the inevitable presence of his real flesh and blood counterparts. The investigation regarding the fictional translator's passing also brings him to the fore and to an inescapable visibility through his translation and evidentiary proofreading/editing marks. In fact, translations, as Susan Bassnett reminds us, "are visible traces of individual readings" (2014, p. 119). "La aventura de las pruebas de imprenta" provides a great way to shed light on the oft-perceived shadowy existence of translators and editors. In addition, this transfictional story offers a unique opportunity to feast one's eyes on the task of these textual sleuths.

References

Arrojo, R. (2018a). Fiction as theory and activism: Rodolfo Walsh's "Footnote". In *Fictional translators: Rethinking translation through literature* (pp. 34-46). Routledge.

Arrojo, R. (2018b). Introduction. In *Fictional translators: Rethinking translation through literature* (pp. 1-16). Routledge.

Bassnettt, S. (2014). *Translation.* Routledge.

Bird, D. W. (2007). Bustos Domecq and the praise of folly. *Variaciones Borges, 23,* 69-83.

Borges, J. L., & Boy-Casares, A. (1998). *Seis problemas para don Isidro Parodi.* Madrid: Alianza Editorial. (Original work published 1942)

Castellino, M. E. (1999). Borges y la narrativa policial: Teoría y práctica. *Revista de Literaturas Modernas, 29,* 89-113.

Cattaneo, P., Green, J., Horowitz, A, Manville, L., & McAuley, S. (Executive Producers). (2022). *Magpie murders.* PBS.

Coldiron, A. E. (2012). Visibility now: Historicizing foreign presences in translation. *Translation Studies, 5*(2), 189-200.

Cruz, L., Durigoni, C., Fain, S., Goldstein, E., Marrone, P., O'Donnell, C., Simonet, L., & Villamagna, G. (Producers). (2015). *Variaciones Walsh* [TV series]. Tranquilo Producciones; TV Pública.

Daniel. (1995). In *Holy Bible: Contemporary English Version* (pp. 1044-1045). American Bible Society.

Doyle, A. C. (2012). Silver blaze. In *The complete Sherlock Holmes: Volume 2* (pp. 3-28). Thomas & Mercer.

Fernández Vega, J. (1997). Más allá de Borges. Una exploración de la temprana narrativa policial de Rodolfo Walsh. *Iberoamericana (1977-2000), 21. Jahrg., 2*(66), 49-69.

Feldman, E., Maci, A. (Writers), & Maci, A. (Director). (2015). *Variciones Walsh* [Motion Picture]. Argentina.

Gamerro, C. (2012). Rodolfo Walsh: Prólogo a una edición nonata de sus "Obras escogidas". *Hispamérica*, 3-14.

Guzmán, M. C. (2013). Translating Latin America: Reading translators' archives. In M. Feltrin-Morris, D. Folaron, & Constanza Guzmán, M. (Eds.), *Translation and Literary Studies: Homage to Marilyn Gaddis Rose* (pp. 90-100). St. Jerome Publishing.

Hakola, O & Kivistö, S. (2014) Introduction: Death in literature. In Outi Hakola and Sari Kivistö (Eds.). *Death in Literature* (pp. vii-xix). Cambridge Scholars Publishing.

Holmes, O. W. (1858). *The autocrat at the breakfast-table*. Houghton, Mifflin and Company.

Holmes, O. W. (1859). *The professor at the breakfast-table*. Houghton, Mifflin and Company.

Holmes, O. W. (1861). *Elsie Venner.* Houghton, Mifflin and Company.

Holmes, O. W. (1867). *The guardian angel*. Houghton, Mifflin and Company.

Holmes, O. W. (1872). *The poet at the breakfast-table*. Houghton, Mifflin and Company.

Holmes, O. W. (1885). *A mortal antipathy*. Houghton, Mifflin and Company.

Holmes, O. W. (1890). *Over the teacups*. Houghton, Mifflin and Company.

Horowitz, A. (2017). *Magpie murders: A novel*. Harper Perennial.

Lowe, E., & Fitz, E. E. (2007). *Translation and the rise of inter-American literature*. University Press of Florida.

Miletich, M. (2022). Ways to (dis)Appear: Dragomans committing suicide in stories by Julio Cortázar and Rodolfo Walsh. *Transletters: International Journal of Translation and Interpreting, 6*, 89-108.

Milkova, S. (2016). The Translator's Visibility or the Ferrante-Goldstein Phenomenon. *Allegoria 73, XXVII*(73), 166-173.

Mossop, B. (2001). *Editing and revising: Revising and editing for translators*. Routledge.

Rabassa, G. (2005). *If this be treason: Translation and its discontents*. New Directions Books.

Schleiermacher, F. (2002). On the different methods of translation. (D. Robinson, Trans.) In D. Robinson (Ed.), *Western translation theory: From Herodotus to Nietzsche.* (pp. 225-238.) St. Jerome. (Original work presented 1813)

Shashok, K. (2001). Author's editors: Facilitators of science information transfer. *Learned Publishing, 14*, 113-121.

Strümper-Krobb, S. (2014). Fictional translators as criminal and detectives. In S. Bayó-Belenguer, E. N. Chuilleanáin, & C. Ó. Cuilleannáin (Eds.), *Translation right or wrong* (pp. 130-139). Four Court Press.

Venuti, L. (1995). *The translator's invisibility: A history of translation*. Routledge.

Walsh, R. (Ed.). (1953). *Diez cuentos policiales argentinos*. Hachette.

Walsh, R. (1972). *Operación masacre*. Ediciones de la Flor. (Original work presented 1957)

Walsh, R. (1977, Marzo 24). *Carta abierta de un escritor a la Junta Militar.* Retrieved from Carta abierta de un escritor a la Junta Militar: https://www. cels.org.ar/common/documentos/CARTAABIERTARODOLFOWALSH.pdf

Walsh, R. (1981a). Asesinato a distancia. In R. Walsh, *Rodolfo Walsh: Obra literaria completa* (pp. 113-157). Siglo XXI Editores.

Walsh, R. (1981b). La aventura de las pruebas de imprenta. In *Rodolfo Walsh: Obra literaria completa* (pp. 11-69). Siglo XXI Editores.

Walsh, R. (1981c) Nota al pie. In *Rodolfo Walsh: Obra literaria completa* (pp. 419-446). Siglo XXI Editores.

Walsh, R. (1981d). *Rodolfo Walsh: Obra literaria completa.* Siglo XXI Editores.

Walsh, R. (1981e). Variaciones en rojo. In R. Walsh, *Rodolfo Walsh: Obra literaria completa* (pp. 71-111). Siglo XXI Editores.

Walsh, R. (1985). Noticia. In *Rodolfo Walsh: Variaciones en rojo* (pp. 6-8). Ediciones de la Flor.

Walsh, R. (1992). Los casos del comisario Laurenzi. In *La máquina del bien y el mal* (pp. 15-95). Clarín /Aguilar.

Wilson, B. (1990). *Gaudi afternoon.* Seal Press.

Wilson, B. (1998). Mi novelista. In *The death of a much-travelled woman and other adventures with Cassandra Reilly* (pp. 195-215). Third Side Press.

Wilson, B. (1998). *The death of a much-travelled woman: and other adventures with Cassandra Reilly.* Third Side Press.

Chapter 6

Translation and Creative Writing: Anita Desai's "Translator Translated"

Sheela Mahadevan

King's College London

Abstract: This chapter examines scenes of writing and translation in a contemporary novella entitled "Translator Translated" (2012b) by Anita Desai. Building on existing research on Transfiction, it investigates what Desai's work reveals about intersections and similarities between translation and creative writing processes. It argues that "Translator Translated" casts light on how and why these processes may overlap and become intertwined in the translator's and writer's career and practice. The chapter also examines what Desai's work reveals about who determines the location and nature of boundaries in literary translation and issues related to the role and ethics of the translator.

Keywords: creative writing, Desai, intersection, transcreation, transgression

***

Introduction

Intersections between translation and creative writing have been the focus of much recent research in translation studies. Scholars have explored various aspects of such entanglements, including the role of literary translation in the careers of writer-translators (Simon, 2007; Woodsworth, 2017, 2018), processes and concepts of self-translation (Cordingley, 2013; Kippur, 2015), and commonalities and interrelations between literary translation and creative writing (Bassnett, 2006; Paz, 1992; Perteghella & Loffredo, 2006; Rossi, 2018a; Rossi, 2018b). Whereas existing studies have frequently explored these intersections through an analysis of the literatures, translations, and lives of translators and writers, this chapter takes an example of transfiction—a term used to refer to fictional depictions of translation, translators, and interpreters[1]—to explore further the intersections and boundaries between translation and creative writing. My focus in this chapter is a novella entitled "Translator Translated" (2012b) by Anita Desai.[2]

Desai is an award-winning writer of English fiction.[3] Although she is not a literary translator, Desai has moved between languages throughout her life.[4] Born to an Indian father and a German mother, she describes her multilingual existence as follows: "I grew up with three languages—we spoke German to our parents, Hindi to our friends and neighbors and, once we went to school, learned to read and write in English" (Bliss, 1988, p. 532). Her multilingualism manifests itself in her writing, which is, on occasion, interspersed with the vocabulary of Indian languages, and which comprises certain English expressions that are inflected by the syntax of Indian languages.[5]

Translation, in various forms, has also played an important role in Desai's career and practice as a writer. Desai was once requested to translate the German letters of an "Austrian Jew living in Calcutta" whose life served as an inspiration for the plotline of her multilingual novel entitled *Baumgartner's Bombay* (1989) (Brush, 1996, p. 277). Desai has also employed other modes of translation in her writing. The novel *In Custody* (1984), for example, comprises various "pseudo-translations" in the form of English versions of Urdu poetry, which are, in fact, pretenses of translated works that do not have originals.[6] Desai has also 'translated' *In Custody* into a film script (Bliss, 1988, p. 533), conceptualizing the transferal of this novel into a film as a process of "translating the literary into the visual medium" (Bliss, 1988, p. 533). Literary translation has also played an important role in the international circulation

---

[1] See Kaindl & Spitzl, 2014. For existing research on 'transfiction,' see Arrojo, 2018; Kaindl, 2021; Maier, 2006; Woodsworth, 2021. For a historical overview of this approach, see Kaindl, 2018, p. 162.

[2] The work was first published in Great Britain in 2011 by Chatto & Windus as a part of a collection of three novellas entitled *The Artist of Disappearance*, and it was simultaneously published in the U.S. in 2011 by Houghton Mifflin Harcourt, Boston as part of a series entitled *The Artist of Disappearance*. It has subsequently been published in various collections, including the following, referred to in this chapter: Anita Desai at *The Artist of Disappearance* (Vintage, 2012a).

[3] Desai was awarded the Sahitya Akademi Award in 1978 for her novel *Fire on the Mountain* and the Guardian Award in 1984 for *The Village by the Sea*. Her novel *In Custody* was shortlisted for the Booker Prize in 1984. See *Meet the author* entry, 1992.

[4] For a self-portrait of the writer's multilingual experiences, see Desai, 2003. For further information on this topic, see Bliss, 1988, pp. 532–533. For an overview of the writer's life and works, see Ho, 2006.

[5] See, for example, the novel *In Custody* (1984). For Desai's description of her multilingual writing, see Bliss, 1988, p. 532.

[6] For further details, see Desai, 2003, p.15.

of Desai's writing; "Translator Translated" along with other works by Desai, was translated into French by Jean-Pierre Aoustin, published in France in 2013 in a collection entitled *L'art de l'effacement* [The Art of Erasure].

"Translator Translated" itself may be described as a "born-translated" work, a term that Rebecca Walkowitz uses to refer to works in which "translation functions as a thematic, structural, conceptual, and sometimes even typographical device" (2015, p. 4). These works, as Walkowitz suggests, "are also frequently *written from translation*. Pointing backward as well as forward, they present translation as a spur to literary innovation, including their own" (2015, p. 4). This phenomenon is exemplified in "Translator Translated," for as Desai herself explains in a preface to one of her works (Desai, 2017a, pp. 9–10), "Translator Translated" is an adaptation and a rewriting of one of her earlier works entitled "The Accompanist" (2017b). "Translator Translated" itself may therefore be considered a translation if translation is understood to be "the most obviously recognizable type of rewriting" (Lefevere, 2016, p. 7). Whereas "Translator Translated" explores the relationship between an author and a translator, "The Accompanist" explores the relationship between a Sitar player and his accompanist, a Tanpura player. There are numerous parallels between the accompanist and the translator in these works. Like the writer who relies on the translator for her voice to be heard in another language, the Sitar player similarly relies on the Tanpura player for his music to be projected. Moreover, both accompanist and translator are frequently overshadowed by the artists whom they support, and both are, to an extent, restricted in their creativity. Concepts and themes of existing work are therefore translated into and transformed in "Translator Translated," and its composition, in which processes of translation and creative writing intersect, foreshadows a central theme of the work itself.

Set in post-independence India, "Translator Translated" depicts the translation and writing experiences and processes of the fictional Indian translator Prema Joshi. The work presents three phases of Joshi's career. In the first phase, Joshi evolves from a failed writer to an English translator of Oriya literature.[7] In the second, she evolves from translator to 'transcreator,'[8]

---

[7] Oriya is a language spoken in Odisha, a region of India. See Pattanaik, 2000 for an overview of the status of Oriya literature, and the importance of English translation for its recognition.

[8] Joshi refers to her translation process as a mode of "transcreation" (Desai, 2012b, p. 84). The term "transcreation" has been defined in various ways in different contexts. It is frequently used to refer to a creative and liberal approach to translation, which involves the embellishment, editing and adaptation of the source text, producing a text which straddles both creative writing and translation. For a discussion of transcreation in the

blurring boundaries between translation and creative writing; in the third, she evolves from 'transcreator' to failed writer.

Desai's work raises several questions which will be explored in relation to the three phases of Joshi's career: what does "Translator Translated" reveal about the ways in which experiences and processes of translating and writing can intersect with, and relate to one another? What motivates the translator to cross the boundaries between translation and creative writing? To what extent can these boundaries be considered to be fluid and elastic, and who dictates their nature and significance?

From failed writer to translator

Prema Joshi did not begin her career as a literary translator, but aspects of this role were already present in her life prior to her adoption of this career, for she divides her time and work between two languages, their literatures, and processes of writing. Before becoming a translator, she attempts to become a published writer and fails. She completes a degree in English literature—the general public perception that English literature has a superior status compared to indigenous language literature in post-independence India is highlighted in the work—yet her true passion lies in the language and literature of Oriya, which is described as her "mother tongue" (Desai, 2012b, p. 49).[9] Owing to the untimely death of her mother, Joshi "lost contact" with this language at an early age (p. 49), and feels compelled to relearn the language and study its literature. In the process, she discovers the works of the fictional writer Suvarna Devi, "the unsung heroine of Oriya letters" (p. 51), and writes a thesis on her works. In order to earn a living, she takes up a job as an English lecturer at a women's college.

Following an unexpected meeting with a former classmate and publisher who outlines her plan to commission English translations of Indian literature composed in indigenous languages, Joshi decides to undertake a translation of Devi's short story collection. She suggests to the publisher that Devi will obtain greater recognition as a result of the translation (p. 58) and she successfully convinces the publisher to include her translation in the new series. The invisibility and precarious status of indigenous language literature of India—both overshadowed by English language and Western literature, and

---

Indian context, see Gopinathan, 2006; Bassnett & Trivedi, 1999; Mukherjee, 1997. For a discussion of transcreation in the Brazilian context, see Vieira, 1999.

[9] Henceforth, page numbers following quotations from "Translator Translated" refer to the edition of the work published in the following volume: *The Artist of Disappearance* (London: Vintage, 2012), as referenced in References.

reliant on English translations to reach a wider audience even within India—is foregrounded in Desai's work.[10]

Joshi also undertakes the translation for personal reasons. It enables her to reconnect with her mother tongue, towards which she feels a sense of "commitment" (p. 59). She considers the reasons for her devotion to the Oriya language and its literature to be a "secret," as she does not reveal this information to the publisher (p. 59). She finds that she can "relieve" herself of the "weight" of this secret through the act of literary translation from Oriya into English (p. 59). Joshi's relationship with her mother tongue mirrors Desai's description of her own relationship with German, her mother tongue. Desai describes the "German strand" of her multilingualism as her "family secret," which she had longed to use in her writing: "I searched for years and years for a subject that would allow me to use German in an Indian setting, the German buried, hidden, locked up within me" (Condé & Philcox, 2003, pp. 15–16). Whereas Joshi reconnects with the Oriya language through the act of literary translation between Oriya and English, Desai finds an opportunity to employ her mother tongue by composing the multilingual work *Baumgartner's Bombay* (1989), which is written primarily in English and is interspersed with German expressions and nursery rhymes.[11] Processes of composing multilingual writing and literary translation appear to be connected to some degree in that they both involve acts of writing between languages, albeit in different ways; moreover, in this context, both processes offer the writer or translator an opportunity to reconnect with their mother tongue and to fulfill a desire to engage with a hidden and unused facet of their multilingualism. Further commonalities between translation and multilingual writing become apparent in the final phase of Joshi's career, as we shall see.

As Joshi translates, she is reminded of her former experience as a failed writer of fiction, which suggests that at a visceral level, processes of creative writing and translation are closely connected. The act of translation also triggers various reflections on the similarities between translation and creative writing processes. Joshi observes that:

---

[10] For a discussion of the role of translation in the circulation of Indian language literatures, see Kamala, 2000, p. 247.
[11] For further details, see Desai, 2003, pp. 15–16. For an analysis of the German nursery rhymes and songs in *Baumgartner's Bombay*, see Stähler, 2010.

Translating Suvarna Devi's words and text into English was not so different [...] from what she herself must have felt when writing them in her own language, which was, after all, a kind of translation too—from seeing and hearing and feeling into syntax [...] The act of translation brought us together [...] as if we were one, two compatible halves of one writer. (pp. 60–61)

Translation and creative writing are therefore presented as related, or "twin processes," as Octavio Paz suggests (1992, p. 160), in that they both involve the transposition of a particular language, sensation or vision into another language. Joshi's description of Devi's writing process echoes Paz's observation that "No text can be completely original because language itself, in its very essence, is already a translation—[...] from the nonverbal world" (1992, p. 154).

Joshi's observation also resonates with the experiences of numerous other writers who conceptualize writing as an act of translation. Caribbean writer Maryse Condé, for example, describes her experience of writing as an act of translating from emotion into word: "I was overcome by an extraordinary emotion caused by the grassy ocean rippling as far as the eye could see [...] I grabbed a pen and notepad and attempted to 'translate' what I was feeling" (2013, p. 96). Similarly, for Argentinian poet Alejandra Pizarnik, as Cecelia Rossi suggests, "the writing process" is seen "as a process which involves some kind of movement or 'translation' from images in the mind to words in a poem on a page" (Rossi 2018b, p. 387). French writer Marcel Proust also suggests that "the duty and task of a writer are the same as those of a translator" (1999, p. 2281),[12] which resonates with the words of French writer Paul Valéry, who argues that: "Writing *anything* at all [...] is a work of translation exactly comparable to that of transmuting a text from one language into another" (1958, p. 299, as cited in Woodsworth, 2018, p. 369).

Not only does Joshi observe that the translation process is similar to that of writing, but her own evolution from writer to translator highlights a particular way in which careers of writing and translating can intersect. Literary translation is presented as a means of renewal and rebirth for the failed writer, who may transform themself into another kind of writer through the act of literary translation. However, although Joshi evolves from failed writer to translator, adopting what she considers to be a "new career" (p. 62), she refers to herself as both "a translator, an author" on multiple occasions (p. 65). Her self-perception appears to be shaped by her former writing experience and ambition; perhaps subconsciously, she secretly still yearns to be and considers herself to be a writer. Her self-perception, which combines the roles

---

[12] This is my translation from the French text.

of writer and translator, becomes a reality, visible in both her practice and theorization of translation in the next phase of her career.

From translator to 'transcreator'

Following her first translation project, Joshi takes on another, translating Devi's second work, a novel, into English. Upon receiving the novel, Joshi finds it "disappointing" (p. 79) compared to the short story collection she had previously translated. As a solution, she decides to modify her translation strategy. Whereas her previous translation methodology had involved restraint, she now adopts a more liberal and creative process:

> I saw that what was needed was for me to be inventive [...] and create a style for the book. So, instead of a literal translation, I decided to take liberties with the text [...] Using Suvarna Devi's text as a basis on which to build, I found I could touch it with small brush strokes of colour and variation [...] And together with this 'enhancement' [...] reduction and deletion were called for too. (pp. 82–83)

Joshi takes on the roles of translator, author, and editor in this project. By editing, omitting, modifying and embellishing certain aspects of the source text, she produces a work which is derivative, and also, to an extent, original.

Joshi's transgression of the conventional boundaries of translation is triggered by various factors.[13] Joshi's adoption of a liberal translation strategy is undertaken consciously and intentionally, guided by her interpretation of the specific source text she is translating. Her desire to improve the source text is partly fueled by her sense of responsibility to uphold the reputations of the multiple agents involved in the translation process, including her own, and that of the publisher and author (p. 80).

It is also possible that Joshi's former writing experience and ambition to become a writer may have influenced her creative translation strategy and imposition of her own style on the source text in this scene. While it is perhaps

---

[13] I use the expression 'conventional boundaries of translation' to refer to those which are frequently adhered to and expected worldwide. The role of the translator is, however, sometimes perceived to be less restrained in the Indian context compared to the Western context. Sujit Mukherjee, for example, notes that "Rupantar (meaning 'change in form') and anuvad ('speaking after' or 'following') are the commonly understood senses of translation in India, and neither term demands fidelity to the original" (2012, p. 90). Mukherjee highlights, however, that the restrictive role of the translator, as is frequently adhered to in the West, also exists in India (2012, p. 89). Joshi employs both approaches in "Translator Translated."

inevitable that the writing practice, styles and aesthetics of any writer will feed into their translation practice in subtle ways, Joshi's work illustrates how a previous writing experience can exert a particularly profound influence on a translator's approach. This approach may consequently involve more creativity than is usually employed in the translation process, and it may involve radical modifications of the source text; as Judith Woodsworth observes:

> Writers [...] when involved in the act of translation, are more inclined to be authorial, or 'author-itative'. [...] In their translational strategies, writers give themselves more freedom and they use their work as translators as a platform for giving voice to their ideas, aesthetics, and personal preoccupations. [...] They stretch the boundaries of the translation proper, and in some cases highjack the act of translation to serve their own ends. (2018, p. 378)

Joshi does, however, have an awareness of the conventional expectations of the translator's role, and she is conscious that she has transgressed the traditional boundaries of literary translation. She worries about whether or not her practice corresponds to her publisher's instructions "to render a faithful translation of Suvarna Devi's work" (p. 83) and is plagued by anxiety owing to her additions to the source text (p. 85).

On other occasions, Joshi considers her practice to be not a transgression of the boundaries of translation but rather, a justifiable stretching and extension of these boundaries. She describes her approach as a "different way of translating" (p. 84), which she defines as "transcreation" (p. 84), and she justifies her methodology by stating "that the best translations are the most inspired, when the translator becomes fully a co-author of the work" (p. 84).

Joshi's description of the translator as co-author resembles that proposed by other translators such as Lori Saint-Martin, who argues that: "Each word that I write is mine, just as it belongs to the author. It seems logical to conclude that the translator is the *co-author of the translated book*" (2022, p. 233).[14] However, the concept of co-authorship has different meanings and implications for the practice of the two translators. For Joshi, co-authorship involves the use of authorial processes—such as the addition of a new style and content to the source text—in the translation process. For Saint-Martin, however, the translator is the co-author of the translated work because she "is the author of her translation, for which she has chosen every word" and because "the words of the translator constitute the work itself" (p. 231), but

---

[14] This is my translation from the French text.

this does not, in her view, justify the addition of new content or a new style to the source text in the translation process. For Saint-Martin, there remains a key difference between the roles and ethics of writer and translator:

> Not imposing one's style or voice: that is the ethics of the translator. Imposing [...] one's style or voice: that is the duty of the writer. In this sense, the writer is free, the translator is not. [...] As a translator, I cannot remove a character or a scene, transform a dialogue or move the position of a chapter; as an author, I can do anything. (p. 231)

For Joshi, then, unlike Saint-Martin, translation involves the fusion of roles of writer and translator in the sense of combining the processes and ethics of both professions. Joshi views this practice as an innovative form of translation, comparing it to other avant-garde artistic movements such as Impressionism, whose novel methodologies she describes as "adventurous" (p. 82).[15] She considers her addition of "small brush strokes of colour and variation" to the source text to resemble the techniques of Impressionist artists (p. 82). Joshi's translation may also be described as 'impressionistic' in other ways; if the Impressionist painters frequently sought to convey an impression rather than every detail of a landscape, so too does Joshi's translation portray an impression of the source text, rather than a literal and detailed depiction of its content.[16] And just as the Impressionist painters' techniques and presence are frequently foregrounded through the inclusion of visible brushstrokes on the canvas, Joshi's translation approach also heightens her visibility as the translator, as discussed later.

Joshi is not alone in defining her radically transformative process as an act of translation. In other contexts, similar works are presented and published as translations. In the Canadian context, for example, Sherry Simon notes that writer-translator Gail Scott's translations of works by "Michael Delisle, Lise Tremblay, and France Théoret [...] read like a combination of the original and a Scott novel" (Lane-Mercier, 2004, cited in Simon, 2006, p. 133), and she observes that "For Scott [...] translation is directed by the same ethical and aesthetic positions as her essays or fiction" (Simon, 2006, p. 133). Simon offers a definition of translation which encompasses such practices that blur boundaries between translation and creative writing, suggesting that translation is "writing that is inspired by the encounter with other tongues, including the effects of creative interference" (2006, p. 17). This definition,

---

[15] For an analysis of innovation in the Impressionist movement, see Ash, 1980, pp. 8–9.
[16] For further details on Impressionist Visual Arts aesthetics, see Ash, 1980, p. 6.

which excludes any notion of fidelity or accuracy, corresponds to the characteristics of Joshi's second translation.

Joshi's process of editing and enhancement also resonates with the thinking and methodology of other translators, including that of David Homel, who argues that "the translation should be better than the original. [...] There is nothing translators like more than correcting 'their' author's mistakes. This is a form of revenge that writers should accept gratefully since it does lead to a better book" (2011, p. 9). Homel (2011, p. 9) notes that his own French translator, Sophie Voillot, performed such an editorial act on his novel entitled *Midway* (2010).

If, like these translators, Joshi considers her liberal, creative, and editorial translation approach to be a justifiable extension and a redrawing of the boundaries of translation, her readers, however, adopt a more critical stance, and maintain a more conventional view of the role of the translator, similar to that of Saint-Martin. Upon publication of the translation, a certain reader considers Joshi's approach to be an unjustifiable transgression of the boundaries of translation, owing to the translator's significant deviations, including the omission of "several pages" from the source text (p. 88). He expresses his criticism to the publisher and thereby influences the latter's opinion of the translation. The publisher prevents any further reprints and apologizes to this reader for mistakes in the translation (p. 88). A number of other readers also express similar concerns, and Joshi's career as a translator, therefore, comes to an abrupt end.

The reception of Joshi's second translation is similar, in some ways, to that of another fictional translator in a work entitled *Vengeance du traducteur* (2009) by French translator-writer Brice Matthieussent, translated into English by Emma Ramadan as *Revenge of the Translator* (2018). Like Joshi, the translator in Matthieussent's work adopts an approach that involves "translating, modifying, correcting, amputating, augmenting, subverting, hijacking, doctoring the source text" (Matthieussent, 2018, p. 70).[17] The translator's editorial intervention is perceived to be an overstepping of the boundaries of translation; the translation is consequently published as an original work of fiction, of which the translator is recognized as the sole author (Matthieussent, 2018, p. 329). Both works by Desai and Matthieussent highlight the extent to which significantly liberal and editorial approaches to

---

[17] Matthieussent's work also casts light on additional factors that may motivate a translator to modify a source text, such as the desire to erase sections which the translator considers to be examples of plagiarism. Other factors are illustrated in *If on a Winter's Night a Traveler* (originally written in Italian) by Italo Calvino. For an analysis of Calvino's work, see Arrojo 2018, pp. 131–150; Simon, 2006, pp. 120–121.

translation are often deemed to be practices that fall outside of the boundaries of translation. For some, these boundaries are rigid and non-negotiable; for others, they are elastic and flexible.

"Translator Translated," then, along with the other works discussed, exposes the complexities of defining the boundaries of translation, a topic that has been discussed in existing studies. Simon, for example, argues that: "If you investigate the wide range of activities that involve translation, and the various degrees of equivalents which we agree to call translations, it becomes evident that the term is an unreliable one" (2006, p. 159) and, as Susan Bassnett observes: "Debates about when a translation stops being a translation and becomes an adaptation have rumbled on for decades, but I have yet to meet anyone who can give me an adequate definition of the difference between the two" (2011, p. 40).[18] Desai not only dramatizes these debates on the boundaries of translation through her portrayal of conflicting perspectives on the topic, but she also offers a distinct contribution to these discussions by exploring the extent to which certain agents connected to the translation may exert a greater authority than others in defining where these boundaries lie, and how flexible they may be.

In the context of Joshi's second translation, it is the bilingual reader with the ability to compare source and target texts (unlike the publisher) who has the greatest influence in determining which works should be circulated under the label of "translation." This differs, then, from Bassnett's view regarding the translator's authority in this matter; she suggests that "when a writer claims that he or she has produced a translation, then I believe that is how we should see it" (2011, p. 41). In Desai's world, the opinion of the translator on this topic is disregarded and muted. Instead, it is those who are involved solely in the reception, rather than the production of the translation, who define the nature and location of the boundaries of translation, thereby determining the fate of the translation and its translator.

From 'transcreator' to failed writer

In the final phase of her artistic career, Joshi relinquishes her role as a translator and undergoes a further process of metamorphosis. Reflecting the title "Translator Translated," Joshi herself is translated and transformed into a new role once again; on this occasion, she is reincarnated as a writer of fiction, attempting to compose "an original work" (p. 90).

Joshi views her engagement with the work of Devi as a form of learning and training for her own writing career, acknowledging that she "owed Suvarna

---

[10] For a further discussion on this topic, see Bassnett, 1998.

Devi a debt for teaching" her how to write (p. 90). Her observation highlights the ways in which a career in literary translation, involving the close reading of the work of another writer, can facilitate the development of writing skills and enhance a career in creative writing. "Translation," as Susan Bassnett observes, "like imitation, can be a means of learning the craft of writing" (2006, p. 174).

However, as Joshi begins to write, she faces various obstacles. A particular aspect of her previous role unexpectedly manifests itself in her writing experience. As a translator, Joshi had constantly wandered between languages, and she continues to switch between her mother tongue and English even as a writer, unintentionally composing a multilingual work. Her experiences of translating and writing are both characterized by a sense of linguistic nomadism. Joshi's experience invites readers to consider the ways in which aspects of a translator's practice and career can seep into and mold their aesthetics and experience as a writer, in uninvited ways.

As she continues to write, Joshi faces another challenge; she realizes to her dismay that her work is haunted by Devi's voice: "I had been writing under her influence, with her voice; it was not mine. In adopting hers, I had lost mine" (p. 91). Joshi's experience resembles that of other writer-translators such as Bassnett, whose writing style is also profoundly influenced by that of a writer whom she had previously translated: "I realized that not only had I stopped translating Pizarnik, but also my whole style of writing had changed, and I was writing not so much like her, but in a style that echoed hers" (2006, p. 181).

While it is true that any writer's work is likely to be influenced, to some degree, by the work of another writer whom they may have translated, Desai's work reveals how a writer's work can be significantly altered by their former translation experience, to the extent that it can even lead to the obliteration of a writer's own voice. Translation is presented, then, as a somewhat destructive force for the writer in "Translator Translated."

Joshi's experience differs from that of other writer-translators, who suggest that translation is beneficial to their writing practice. Jhumpa Lahiri, for example, suggests that translation "shows me how to work with new words, how to experiment with new styles and forms, how to take greater risks, how to structure and layer my sentences in different ways" (2022, p. 7). She also suggests that there is a reciprocal process of nourishment between acts of translation and creative writing, conceptualizing "writing and translation as two aspects of the same activity, two faces of the same coin, or maybe two strokes exercising distinct but complementary strengths, that allow me to swim greater distances" (2022, p. 8). Desai's work, however, reveals that these two modes of writing are not always complementary but can also be detrimental to one another: the overexercising of the writer's skills in the translation process can lead to the downfall of the translator, and when a writer translates the work of another, this experience can subsequently generate undesired aesthetics and experiences in the writing process.

Unsettled and discouraged by this writing experience, Joshi abandons her attempt to become a writer and returns to her former status as a failed writer. Joshi's endeavors to become word artists of different kinds—translator and writer—therefore both meet with disaster. Moreover, the evaporation of her artistic career is reflected in the title of one of the collections of Desai's novellas: *The Artist of Disappearance* (2012), which includes the work "Translator Translated," along with two other novellas relating to art.

Conclusion

What does "Translator Translated" reveal about intersections between translation and creative writing and the nature of boundaries in literary translation? On the one hand, the work foregrounds the fluidity of these boundaries by illustrating how processes of writing and translation are frequently combined, either intentionally or unintentionally, and to greater or lesser degrees, in the work of both translators and writers. Joshi's translation of Devi's novel and her own work of fiction are both translational—here, I employ Simon's definition of the term 'translational writing' as "the zones where creative writing and translation mesh" (2012, p. 8)—for she intentionally combines these modes of writing in her translation of Devi's novel, and she unintentionally translates Devi's voice into her own creative writing, reflecting the notion that "translation is often indistinguishable from creation; [...] there is constant interaction between the two, a continuous, mutual enrichment" (Paz, 1992, p. 160). On the other hand, "Translator Translated" reminds us that rigid boundaries in the act of literary translation persist in the minds of certain stakeholders, even if the translator imagines that these boundaries may be malleable and porous. Above all, the work reminds us how important *readership* can be when it comes to determining the nature and location of boundaries in literary translation.

"Translator Translated" is also revelatory of the ways in which the linguistic framework of the readership may influence their evaluation of the translation. A monolingual reader, or a reader who cannot compare the source and target texts, will be unaware of any differences between them. A bilingual reader with a knowledge of the languages of the source and translated texts, in contrast, may compare the two versions and observe differences between them, using these as a criterion by which to judge whether or not a translator has transgressed the boundaries of translation. Of course, any translation involves the transformation of the source text, and no translation can be entirely identical or directly equivalent to a source text owing to linguistic and cultural differences between source and target texts, but if boundary violations in the act of translation are determined by *radical* modifications and differences, such as the significant omission and addition of content, as exemplified in "Translator Translated," then the visibility of such violations are, in turn, to an extent dependent on the linguistic framework of the readership.[19]

If the visibility of such transgressions is determined by the linguistic framework of the readership, it is important to note that the linguistic framework of the readership can also influence the translator's perception of their task. Gayatri Chakravorty Spivak touches on this when discussing the differences between translating into English the French writing of Jacques Derrida and the Bengali writing of Mahasweta Devi for a U.S. readership. Spivak explains:

> When I translated Jacques Derrida's *De la grammatologie*, I was reviewed in a major journal for the first and last time. In the case of my translations of Devi, I have almost no fear of being accurately judged by my readership here. It makes the task more dangerous and more risky. And that for me is the real difference between translating Derrida and translating Mahasweta Devi. (2012, p. 321)

An analysis of other translator testimonials and fictional depictions of translators would cast light on the ways in which the translator's awareness of the linguistic framework of their readership(s) may influence their approach, in addition to other factors that may motivate the translator to cross the boundaries between translation and creative writing.

References

Arrojo, R. (2018). *Fictional translators: Rethinking translation through literature.* Routledge.

Ash, R. (1980). *The impressionists and their Art.* Orbis Publishing.

Bassnett, S. (1998). When is a translation not a translation? In S. Bassnett & A. Lefevere (Eds.), *Constructing cultures: Essays on literary translation* (pp. 25–40). Multilingual Matters.

Bassnett, S. (2006). Writing and translating. In S. Bassnett & P. R. Bush (Eds.), *The translator as writer* (pp. 173–183). Continuum.

Bassnett, S. (2011). *Reflections on translation.* Channel View Publications.

---

[19] This, of course, depends on whether the bilingual reader decides to compare source and target texts. In "Translator Translated," it is not clear as to whether the author Devi, who can read in both Oriya and English, compares the two versions. She only comments on the appearance of the book, rather than on the translation itself (p. 89).

Bassnett, S., & Trivedi, H. (1999). Introduction. In S. Bassnett & H. Trivedi (Eds.), *Post-colonial translation: Theory & practice* (pp. 1–18). Routledge.

Bliss, C. D. (1988). *Against the current: A conversation with Anita Desai. 29*(3), 521–537.

Brush, P. (1996). German, Jew, foreigner: The immigrant experience in Anita Desai's Baumgartner's Bombay. *Berghahn Books, 8*(3), 227–285.

Calvino, I. (1992). *If on a winter's night a traveller* (W. Weaver, Trans.). Vintage. (Original work published 1979)

Condé, M., & Philcox, R. (2013). Intimate enemies: A conversation between an author and her translator. In K. Batchelor & C. Bisdorff (Eds.), *Intimate Enemies: Translation in Francophone Contexts* (pp. 89–97). Liverpool University Press.

Cordingley, A. (Ed.). (2013). *Self-Translation: Brokering originality in hybrid culture.* Bloomsbury Publishing.

Desai, A. (1989). *Baumgartner's Bombay.* Penguin.

Desai, A. (1999a). *Fire on the mountain.* Vintage.

Desai, A. (1999b). *In custody.* Vintage. (Original work published 1984)

Desai, A. (2001). *The village by the sea.* Puffin.

Desai, A. (2003). Various lives. In I. De Courtviron (Ed.), *Lives in translation: Bilingual writers on identity and creativity* (pp. 11–18). Palgrave Macmillan.

Desai, A. (2012a). *The artist of disappearance.* Vintage.

Desai, A. (2012b). Translator translated. In *The artist of disappearance* (pp. 41–92). Vintage.

Desai, A. (2013). *L'art de l'effacement: Trois nouvelles* (J.-P. Aoustin, Trans.). Mercure de France. (Original work published 2011)

Desai, A. (2017a). Preface. In *The complete stories* (pp. 7–10). Chatto and Windus.

Desai, A. (2017b). The accompanist. In *The complete stories* (pp. 51–62). Vintage. (Original work published 1975)

Gopinathan, G. (2006). Translation, transcreation and culture: Theories of translation in Indian languages. In T. Hermans (Ed.), *Translating Others* (pp. 236–246). St. Jerome.

Ho, E. Y. L. (2006). *Anita Desai.* British Council.

Homel, D. (2010). *Midway.* Cormorant Books.

Homel, D. (2011). I can do better than that! *TranscUlturAl: A Journal of Translation and Cultural Studies, 4*(1), 5–14.

Kaindl, K. (2018). The remaking of the translator's reality. In J. Woodsworth (Ed.), *The fictions of translation* (pp. 157–170). John Benjamins.

Kaindl, K. (2021). (Literary) Translator studies: Shaping the field. In K. Kaindl, W. Kolb, & D. Schlager (Eds.), *Literary translator studies* (pp. 1–38). John Benjamins.

Kaindl, K., & Spitzl, K. (Eds.). (2014). *Transfiction: research into the realities of translation fiction.* John Benjamins.

Kamala, N. (2000). Gateway of India: Representing the nation in English translation. In S. Simon & P. St - Pierre (Eds.), *Changing the terms: Translating in the postcolonial era* (pp. 245–260). University of Ottawa Press.

Kippur, S. (2015). *Writing it twice: Self-Translation and the making of a world literature in French.* Northwestern University Press.

Lahiri, J. (2022). *Translating myself and others*. Princeton University Press.

Lane-Mercier, G. (2004). Helen with a secret, de Michael Delisle. *Spirale, 197*(19).

Lefevere, A. (2016). *Translation, rewriting, and the manipulation of literary fame*. Routledge.

Maier, C. (2006). The Translator as theôros: Thoughts on cogitation, figuration and current creative writing. In T. Hermans (Ed.), *Translating others (volume 1)* (pp. 163–180). St. Jerome.

Matthieussent, B. (2009). *Vengeance du traducteur*. P.O.L.

Matthieussent, B. (2018). *Revenge of the translator* (E. Ramadan, Trans.). Deep Vellum. (Original work published 2009)

Meet the Author Anita Desai. (1992). Sahitya Akademi. https://sahitya-akademi.gov.in/library/meettheauthor/anita_desai.pdf. Sahitya Akademi & India International Centre.

Mukherjee, S. (1997). Transcreating translation: An Indian mode. *Kunapipi, 19*(3), 85–93.

Mukherjee, S. (2012). *Translation as discovery and other essays on Indian literature in English translation* (e-book). Orient Blackswan Private Limited.

Pattanaik, D. (2000). The power of translation: A survey of translation in Orissa. In S. Simon & P. St-Pierre (Eds.), *Changing the terms: Translating in the postcolonial era* (pp. 71–86). Ottawa University Press.

Paz, O. (1992). Translation: literature and letters. In J. Biguenet & R. Schulte (Eds.), (I. Del Corral, Trans.), *Theories of translation: An anthology of essays from Dryden to Derrida* (pp. 152–162). University of Chicago Press. (Original work published 1971)

Perteghella, M. & Loffredo, E. (Eds.). (2006). *Translation and creativity: Perspectives on creative writing and translation studies*. Continuum.

Proust, M. (1999) *À la recherche du temps perdu*. J-Y Tadié (Ed.), Gallimard. (Original work published 1913-1927)

Rossi, C. (2018a). Literary translation and disciplinary boundaries: Creative writing and interdisciplinarity. In K. Washbourne & B. Van Wyke (Eds.), *The Routledge handbook of literary translation* (pp. 42–57). Routledge.

Rossi, C. (2018b). Translation as a creative force. In S-A. Harding & O. C. Cortes (Eds.), *Routledge handbook of translation and culture* (pp. 381–397). Routledge.

Saint-Martin, L. (2022). *Un bien nécessaire: Éloge de la traduction littéraire*. Boréal.

Simon, S. (2006). *Translating Montreal: Episodes in the life of a divided city*. McGill-Queen's University Press.

Simon, S. (2007). 'A single brushstroke', writing through translation. *In Translation – Reflections, Refractions, Transformations*, 107–116. https://doi.org/10.1075/btl.71.13sim

Simon, S. (2012). *Cities in translation: Intersections of language and memory*. Routledge.

Spivak, G. C. (2012). The politics of translation. In L. Venuti (Ed.), *The translation studies reader* (3rd ed., pp. 312–330). Routledge.

Stähler, A. (2010). The holocaust in the nursery: Anita Desai's 'Baumgartner's Bombay'. *Journal of Postcolonial Writing, 26*(1), 76–88.

Valéry, P. (1958). Variations on the eclogues. In J. Mathews (Ed.), (D. Folliot, Trans.), *The art of poetry* (Vol. 7). Routledge and Kegan Paul. (Original work published 1953)

Vieira, E. (1999). Liberating Calibans: Readings of antropofagia and Haroldo de Campos' poetics of transcreation. In S. Bassnett & H. Trivedi (Eds.), *Post-Colonial translation: theory and practice* (pp. 95–113). Routledge.

Walkowitz, R. L. (2015). *Born translated: The contemporary novel in an age of world literature*. Columbia University Press.

Woodsworth, J. (2017). *Telling the story of translation: Writers who translate*. Bloomsbury.

Woodsworth, J. (2018). Writers as translators. In K. Washbourne & B. Van Wyke (Eds.), *The Routledge handbook of literary translation* (pp. 369–381). Routledge.

Woodsworth, J. (2021). Dressing up for Halloween: Walking the line between translating and writing. In K. Kaindl, W. Kolb, & D. Schlager (Eds.), *Literary Translator Studies* (pp. 293–306). Benjamins.

Afterthoughts

Marko Miletich

SUNY Buffalo State University

"Fiction is the lie that tells the truth, after all."

Neil Gaiman

The writers in this volume have shared their transfictional musings with the intention of providing fresh perspectives on using fiction to discuss issues related to translation studies and the everyday work of translators. The fictional tales on which these chapters are based illustrate how translation/interpreting and the work of flesh and blood translators/interpreters have a global impact and are necessary to advance the exchange and circulation of ideas and culture. Fiction itself serves as a "semiotic mechanism for the construction of alternate universes" (Margolin, 1990, p. 455). The characters who inhabit those fictional "alternate" worlds are often very similar to the people encountered through everyday "real world" interactions. Their fictional representations invite reflection on some of the preconceived notions about them, their professions, and the challenges they may face while performing their duties. Although their presence is likely to be overlooked, their existence can easily be ascertained.

The chapters in this volume have shown that fictional interpreters, translators, and their work share asymmetrical contexts, presenting many challenges (as do their real-life counterparts). The authors in this collection have described how language, as the basis of translatorial activity, is a significant marker of identity and, as such, it is often garnered in fiction to represent its use (and abuse) by language professionals. These authors have examined how the nostalgia for a pre-Babylonian language can lead to yearning for a protolanguage, whereby translation and interpreting become unnecessary. These essays evaluated how indispensable interlingual oral language facilitators, known as interpreters (one of the oldest professions in the world) may often display agency as a conscious will to help despite ethical concerns and regardless of societal expectations. In addition, this collection has studied how these modern fictional dragomans struggle with ethical dilemmas and often wrestle with having to interpret for an unrighteous other.

Besides reflections on the circumstances of oral communication, the authors gathered here have illustrated how written language professionals (translators and editors) are indispensable to ensuring the flow of ideas as they leave their indelible mark while providing texts with an "afterlife" (in the Benjaminian sense)[1]. Finally, these chapters have explored the intersections between writing and translation (since translation is seen as a form of creative writing).

As interpreters traverse linguistic and pragmatic territories, they are relegated to an imposed invisibility and a subservient, derivative role. As Theo Hermans (2002) reminds us, interpreters' utterances do not refer to themselves, and yet they are the ones making those very utterances (p. 12). Interpreters provide in one language what someone is saying in another. They provide the ideas and expressions of others, but they "interpret" by carefully and consciously selecting their words to provide meaning. Their linguistic choices and physical proximity, however, confirms their existence as active participants in the transfer of information, regardless of the power dynamics that accompany every interpreter-mediated event.

This visibility is shared by translators who inevitably leave traces of their translatorial action. Unlike interpreters, translators do not have a physical presence. In addition, translators are supposed to be "a wholly discreet, transparent, disenfranchised mediator" (Hermans, 2002, p.11). Translators, however, intervene, as two of the chapters have demonstrated, and are fully enfranchised, be it by using translatorial strategies, by purposely adding to a source text, by omitting words or phrases considered dispensable or using paratextual devices. Translators are world travelers who bring textual souvenirs from foreign lands.

Throughout this volume, several areas of research have been identified. Future research may concentrate on the interdisciplinarity of translation studies and its relationship with various disciplines. The issue of gender has been discussed (specifically female interpreters vs. male clients and interpreting as a feminized occupation), although further research may be conducted to determine gendered representation of interpreters and translators, taking into consideration the close relationship between gender studies and translation studies (both deal with binaries male/female, original translation/ heterosexual/homosexual, author/translator, etc.). Another area of interest for future exploration may be the corporeality of translation and interpreting. Although translation and interpreting have traditionally been

---

[1] Walter Benjamin discusses how translations provides a life after an original: "a translation issues from the original – not so much for its life as from its afterlife" (2002, p. 76).

viewed as purely intellectual endeavors, they, in fact, require a human body.[2] Translators need to be able to use their eyes to read and decipher the symbols on the printed page, and in the case of persons with vision impairment or low vision, translators need either their fingers to read Braille or their ears to listen to an Optical Character Recognition (OCR) system. Interpreters need their ears to hear what is to be subsequently transmitted, and in the case of deaf and hard of hearing, the body is also used through sign language. The traditional rules imposed on translators and interpreters reflect a distinguishable somatophobia, a neglecting of the body as a partner in decision-making. Following Douglas Robinson (1991), who proposes a somatic approach to language, transfictional stories can help translators and interpreters relate, through borrowed fictional bodies, to the corporeality inherent in their professional roles even as they struggle to accomplish their tasks.

This volume has focused on fictional representations of translation and interpreting phenomena. Transfictional stories can help to understand preconceived notions about translation and the roles of translators and interpreters. As shown in the tales discussed in this collection, well-crafted storytelling can enlighten and provoke reflection about translation and the translators and interpreters who communicate an alterity otherwise impossible to attain. Just as fiction awakens readers to alternate possibilities and may influence their actual thoughts and daily activities, transfiction can make readers aware of the importance of translatorial action and the language professionals who provide alterity created in a foreign land.

As this volume has hopefully demonstrated, fictional translations and transfictional beings can generate awareness of issues that relate to human existence through a nonexistent world that is not only enjoyable to read but also offers reflection on accepted everyday truths and appreciation of the multilingual and translatorial world humans irremediably inhabit.

References

Benjamin, W. (2002). The task of the translator: An introduction to the translation of Baudelaire's Tableaux Parisiens. In L. Venuti (Ed.), *The translation studies reader* (H. Zhon, Trans., pp. 75-83). Routledge.

Gaiman, N. (2016). *The view from the cheap seats.* William Morrow.

---

[2] At least for now. The progress of artificial intelligence (AI) and the advances in machine translation/machine interpreting may replace human translators and interpreters altogether in a not-too-distant future. Humans may still be needed but perhaps only in a post-editing capacity.

Hermans, T. (2002). Paradoxes and aporias in translation and translation studies. In A. Riccardi (Ed.), *Translation studies: Perspectives on an emerging discipline* (pp. 10-23). Cambridge University Press.

Margolin, U. (1990). The what, the when, and the how of being a character in literary narrative. *Style, 24*(3), 453-468.

Robinson, D. (1991). *The translator's turn.* The John Hopkins University Press.

Index

A

activism, 30, 31
agency, xix, 18, 23, 25, 27, 32, 36, 37, 39, 53, 105
AIIC (Association International des Interprètes de Conférence), 37
Alighieri, Dante, 13
Angelelli, Claudia, 45, 47
Arrojo, Rosemary, xvi, 26, 30, 31, 38, 52, 64, 79, 83, 88, 96
artificial intelligence (AI), 107
Ash, Russel, 95
Ayan, Irem, 38, 41, 45, 61, 64

B

Bâ, Amadou Hampâté, 18
Bachmann, Ingeborg, 36
Baer, Brian, 52
Baker, Mona, 62
Baker, Mona & Maier, Carol, 38
Bassnett, Susan, 84, 87, 90, 97, 98
Beaton, Morven, 40
Beebee, Thomas, 52
Ben-Ari, Nitsa, 28, 30
Benigni, Roberto, 36
Benjamin, Walter, 4, 10, 12, 106
Berman, Antoine, 8
Bielsa, Esperança, 55
Bioy Casares, Adolfo, 70
Bird, David, 70
Bliss, Corrine Demas, 88
Borges, Jorge Luis, xviii, 52, 70
    "Pierre Menard, Author of the Quixote", xviii, 52

Bourdieu, Pierre, 41
Brooke-Rose, Christine, 36
Brush, Pippa, 88

C

Calvino, Italo, xviii, 2, 96
    If on a Winter's Night a Traveler, xviii, 2, 96
Camayd-Freixas, Erik, 47
Carstensen, Gunilla & Dahlberg, Leif, 44, 45
Castellino, Marta Elena, 73
Cattaneo, Peter, 74
Center for Inter-American Relations, 77
Cervantes, Miguel de, xviii
    Don Quixote, xviii
Chamberlain, Lori, xvi
Chesterman, Andrew, 26
Claramonte, Carmen África Vidal, 44
Coldiron, Anne, 78
Condé, Maryse, 92
Coppola, Sofia, 36
Cordingley, Anthony, 87
Cortázar, Julio, 12, 52
Cox, Michael, 36
Cronin, Michael, 36, 52
Cruz, Lorena, 71
Cypess, Sandra Messinger, 22, 23

D

Daniel, 69, 75, 76, 80, 83
deformazione professionale, 10
Del Castillo, Adelaida, 21, 29
del Castillo, Bernal Díaz, 20, 23

Delabastita, Dirk & Grutman,
    Rainier, 52
Delisle, Jean & Woodsworth,
    Judith, 23
Delisle, Michael, 95
Desai, Anita, xxi, 87, 88, 89, 90, 91,
    96, 97, 98, 99
    Baumgartner's Bombay, 88, 91
    Fire on the Mountain, 88
    In Custody, 88
    The Accompanist, 89
    The Artist of Disappearance, 90
    The Village by the Sea, 88
    Translator, Translated, xxi, 88,
        89, 90, 93, 97, 98, 99, 100, 101
detective, xviii, xix, xx, xxi, 46, 47,
    65, 69, 70, 71, 72, 73, 74, 80, 81,
    82, 83
Diriker, Erbu, 57, 64
Downie, Jonathan, 27, 28
Doyle, Sir Arthur Conan, 70, 72
Duranti, Francesca, 2

E

Echo, xxii
editor, xxi, 70, 71, 74, 80, 83, 93
    editors and proofreaders, 70, 75,
        80, 82, 83
editorial, 96
Elias-Bursać, Ellen, 60
Esperanto, 3
Esquivel, Laura, 23
ethics, xix, xx, 17, 25, 43, 46, 47, 62,
    87, 95
ethnographic fiction, 37, 48
European External Action Service
    (EEAS), 2

F

Feldman, Ester, 71

Fernández Vega, José, 81
fidelity, 4, 28, 37, 53, 54, 55, 83, 93,
    96
First International Conference on
    Fictional Translators in
    Literature and Film, xvii
Florentine Codex, 20
French, xix, 8, 14, 56, 59, 89, 92, 94,
    96, 100
Fuentes, Carlos, xviii, 22, 29
    The Two Shores, xviii, 22, 29

G

Gaiba, Francesca, 60
Gaiman, Neil, 105
Gamerro, Carlos, 82
gender, xv, 38, 106
gendered, xx, 36, 39, 40, 41, 42, 43,
    46, 106
gendered and racialized labor, 37
Gentile, Paola, 41
Glass, Suzanne, 29
Godayol, Pilar, 19, 22, 24
Gopinathan Gayatri, 90
Goscinny, René & Uderzo, Albert,
    36
Gramsci, Antonio, 40
Guzmán, María Constanza, 55, 77

H

Hagedorn, Hans Christian, xviii
Hakola, Outi & Kivistö, Sari, 78
Hale, Sandra Beatriz, 58
Hermans, Theo, xvi, 106
Hermes, 74
Herrera, Yuri, xx, 17, 19, 23, 24, 27,
    28, 32
    *Signs Preceding the End of the
        World*, xx, 17, 19, 27, 32
Hindi, xxi, 88

Hoagland, Sarah Lucia, 39
Hochschild, Arlie Russell, 39, 41, 44
Hokkanen, Sari, 64
Holmes, Oliver Wendell, 70, 76, 79
  A Mortal Antipathy, 70
  Elsie Venner, 70
  Over the Teacups, 70
  The Autocrat at the Breakfast-Table, 70
  The Guardian Angel, 70
  The Poet at the Breakfast-Table, 70, 76
  The Professor at the Breakfast-Table, 70
Holmes, Sherlock, 36, 69, 72
Homel, David, 96
Hubscher-Davidson, Severine, 61

I

Immigration and Naturalization Service (INS Service), 47
infidelity, xviii, 36, 82
(in)fidelity, xix, 18, 52, 53
Inghilleri, Moira, 41, 44, 53
International Criminal Court, xx, 55, 56
interpreter, xvi, xviii, 45, 46, 47, 48, 52, 53, 55, 56, 57
  conference interpreter, 53
  fictional interpreter, xix, xx, 2, 18, 36, 51, 52, 53, 56, 58, 64, 105
  interpreter/mistress, 56
  interpreter's agency, 31, 53
  simultaneous interpreter, 11
interpreting, xvi, xx, xxi, 1, 18, 19, 20, 21, 25, 26, 27, 28, 29, 30, 32, 36, 37, 38, 39, 40, 41
  chuchotage, 58

codes of ethics, 18, 19, 26, 27, 28, 29, 35, 36, 47
consecutive interpreting, 45
court interpreting, 37, 38, 44
depositions, xx, 37, 41, 43, 45, 48
machine interpreting, 107
non-interpreting, 28
simultaneous interpreting, 58
intersection, xvii, xxi, 87, 99
intimacy, 57, 58, 59, 63, 64
invisibility, xxi, 20, 25, 27, 32, 36, 37, 38, 48, 60, 74, 78, 79, 90, 106
(in)visibility, xix, 52, 53, 55, 64, 84
invisibilize, 81
Italian, xix, 2, 4, 5, 8, 9, 10, 14, 96

J

Jager, Rebecca, 21
Jansen, Hanne, 57
Japanese, 39, 56, 61
Jerome, 9, 15, 74
Jerónimo de Aguilar, xviii, 22
Joliff, Tatiana Calderón, 30

K

Kaindl, Klaus, xvi, 35, 52
Kaindl, Klaus & Spitzl, Karlheinz, 26, 88
Kamala, N, 91
Karttunen, Frances, 19, 23, 25
Kim, Suki, xx, 35, 36, 37, 38, 39, 40, 41, 42, 43, 46, 47, 48
  The Interpreter, xix, xx
Kippur, Sara, 87
Kitamura, Katie, xx, 36, 51, 53, 54, 55, 56, 57, 58, 60, 61, 62, 63, 64
  Intimacies, xx, 36, 53, 55, 56, 58, 64

Korean, 35, 38, 39, 40, 42, 43, 44,
    45, 46, 47
Koskinen, Kaisa, 57, 59, 61
Kosztolányi, Dezsö, xviii
    "Kornél Esti", xviii
Kurosawa, Akira, 7
Kurz, Ingrid, 18, 26, 28, 36, 53

L

La Malinche, xviii, xx, 19, 32, 43, 56
Lahiri, Jhumpa, 98
Lane-Mercier, Gillian, 95
le Carré, John, 29
Leal, Alice, 52
Lefevere, André, 89
Levy, Shawn, 7
linguists, 3, 5, 7
Lodge, David, 7
Lowe, Elizabeth & Fitz, Earl, 77

M

Maier, Carol, 64, 88
Malinche-esque, xx, 17, 20, 23, 27,
    32
Marani, Diego, xix, 1, 2, 3, 5, 6, 9,
    10, 11, 12, 13, 14
    New Finnish Grammar, xix, 1, 2,
        5, 14, 15
    The Interpreter, 2, 10, 14
    The Last of the Vostyachs, xix, 2,
        5, 14
Margolin, Uri, 105
Marías, Javier, xviii, 36
    A Heart so White, xviii, 36
Matthieussent, Brice, 96
Meet the author, 88
Miletich, Marko, xvi, xx, xxi, 52, 79
Milkova, Stiliana, 78
Monacelli, Claudia, 41
Morris, Ruth, 44

Mossop, Brian, 82
Mukherjee, Sujit, 90, 93

N

NAJIT (National Association of
    Judiciary Interpreters and
    Translators), 37, 50
National Council on Interpreting
    in Health Care, 34
Northeast Modern Language
    Association, NeMLA, xiii, xvii

O

Optical Character Recognition
    (OCR), 107
Oriya, xix, xxi, 89, 90, 91, 100

P

Pagano, Adriana, xvii, 52
Parkert, Cecilia, 53
Pattanaik, Diptiranjan, 89
Paz, Octavio, 21, 22, 87, 92, 99
personal "I", xx, 57, 58, 61
Perteghella, Manuela & Loffredo,
    Eugenia, 87
Pirandello, Luigi, x, 12
Ponce, Nestor, 29
printing proofs, xxi, 69, 72, 80, 81,
    82
proofreader/editor, 81
proofreaders, 75, 83
proofreading/editing marks, 75,
    80, 84
Proust, Marcel, 92
Pym, Anthony, 57

Q

Quine, Richard, 40

R

Rabassa, Gregory, 77
Rafael, Vicente, 9
Rhee, Suk Koo, 42, 46
Rivero, Giovanna, 24
Robinson, Douglas, 107
Rossi, Cecilia, 87, 92
Ryan, Rachel, 41

S

Saint-Martin, Lori, 94, 95, 96
Schleiermacher, Friederich, 78
Schmidt, Nancy, 37
Schopohl, Eva, 36
Scliar, Moacyr, 52
Seneca, xv
Shashok, Karen, 82
Shlesinger, Miriam, 26
Simon, Sherry, 36, 43, 87, 95, 96, 97, 99
somatophobia, 107
Spanish, xix, 19, 21, 23, 24, 56, 76, 77, 79
Spanish conquest, 22
Spânu, Liliana, 41
Spitzl, Karlheinz, xvii, xxiii, 18, 28, 35, 51
Spivak, Gayatri Chakravorty, 57, 100
Staël, Madame de, 8
Stähler, Axel, 91
Stahuljak, Zrinka, 44
Steiner, George, xviii, 9, 52
Strümper-Krobb, Sabine, 52, 72
subversion, 42
suicide, 4, 80, 81

T

Tabucchi, Antonio, 2

Takeda, Kayoko, 53, 61
Tate, G. & Turner, Graham, 19
Tate, Julee, 23
Tawada, Yoko, 52
The National Council on Interpreting in Health Care [NCIHC], 26
Thiem, Jon, 52
Todorova, Maria, 18, 28
transcreation, 89, 90, 94
transcreator, 90, 93, 97
transfiction, xv, xvi, xvii, xviii, 18, 24, 28, 30, 51, 52, 87, 88
transfictional, xv, xvi, xxii, 51, 53, 65, 71, 77, 79, 83, 84
transfictionality, xv
transgression, 36, 37, 42, 93, 94, 96
translation, xviii, 71, 89, 91, 92, 93, 94, 98, 99, 106, 107
  machine translation, 107
  translation and creative writing, xxi, 87, 88, 89, 90, 91, 92, 95, 98, 99, 100
translator, xxi, 70, 71, 73, 74, 77, 78, 79, 80, 81, 91, 92, 93, 94, 95, 96, 97, 98, 99, 100, 105, 106, 107
  fictional translator, xviii, 52, 54, 75, 76, 77, 78, 80, 81, 82, 84, 96
  translator as co-author, 94
  translator/editor, 69, 70
  translator's authority, 97
  translators and detectives, 69, 71, 73, 74
  translators and editors, 69, 71, 84, 106
  translators and interpreters, xv, xvi, xvii, xviii, xix, xxii, 1, 2, 18, 20, 30, 35, 37, 52, 62, 64, 72, 105, 107
  translators and writers, 99

translatorial, xvi, xvii, xix, xxii, 51, 71, 74, 76, 77, 78, 83, 105, 106, 107

U

Ursprache, 10, 12

V

Valdeón, Roberto, 21, 22, 56
Valéry, Paul, 92
Venuti, Lawrence, 6, 25, 37, 78, 79
   The Translator's Invisibility: A History of Translation, 6, 25, 78
Vieira, Else, xvii, 90
visibility, xxi, 1, 17, 19, 20, 23, 26, 32, 52, 56, 58, 59, 69, 74, 75, 80, 82, 84, 95, 100, 106
   visibility versus invisibility, 26, 27, 84
von Flotow, Louise, 43

W

Wadensjö, Cecilia, 64
Wakabayashi, Judy, 52
Walkowitz, Rebecca, 89
Walsh, Rodolfo, xx, 30, 52, 69, 70, 71, 72, 74, 75, 76, 77, 78, 79, 80, 82, 83, 84
   "Asesinato a distancia", 70, 71

"Carta abierta de un escritor a la Junta Militar", 71
"La aventura de las pruebas de imprenta", 70, 71
"La máquina del bien y el mal", 71
   Los casos del comisario Laurenzi, 71
   Obra literaria completa, 71
   Operación Masacre, 71
   Variaciones en rojo, 70
   Variaciones Walsh, 71
Wilson, Barbara, xviii, 73, 74
   Gaudí Afternoon, xviii
   "Mi novelista", 74
   The Death of a Much-Travelled Woman and Other Adventures with Cassandra Reilly, 74
Wilson, Rita, xvi, 52
Woodsworth, Judith, xvii, 25, 87, 88, 92, 94
writer-translators, 98

Y

Yoshimoto, Banana, xviii
   NP, xviii

Z

Zunshine, Lisa, xv
Zwischenberger, Cornelia, 40

www.ingramcontent.com/pod-product-compliance
Lightning Source LLC
Chambersburg PA
CBHW062041270326
41929CB00014B/2493